THE CREDO

DOUG MCPHILLIPS

2
Other Visionary Stories

NOVELS

From Darkness to Light.
The Sword of Discernment.
Santiago Traveller.
I, Prophet.
Awake to my Gutted Dream.
We is Me Upside Down.
The Guru of Jerusalem
Masters at my table.
The Wicklow Way.
The Adventures of Ace McDice,
Stretch Deed & Moonshine Melody.
Instant karma & Grace.
Reflections of an Old Man

Country Camino. Album
Santiago Traveller. Album
Soul Fact. Album

Doug McPhillips 2023.

ISBN 978-0-6454221-4-6

This book is copyright. Apart from any fair dealing for the purpose of private study, research, criticism or reviews permitted under the Copyright Act, no part may be reproduced by any process whatsoever without the editor's permission.

National Library of Australia Catalog-in-publication data:
Holy Bible, New International Version 1980 edition.
HolyBible, Revised Standard 1989 edition.
Pilgrimage, Mark K.Shriver, Random House, New York,2 016.
Catechism of the Catholic Church-Society of St. Paul, 1994.
Excerpts from Code of Canon Law, Canon Law Society, 1983.
Excerpts from Vatican Council 11 Documents, 1992 editions.

Forward:

This book presents a layman's point of view of the essentials and fundamentals of the Catholic faith; its doctrines of belief and morals, symbolisms and signs that embrace the teachings of the church pre and post the Second Vatican Council (1962-1964).

It calls for a profession of faith that is not necessarily in accord with human opinion but of what has been gathered from the Scriptures, to present the teaching of the faith in its entirety. It is a summary of faith encompassing in a few words the whole knowledge of the true religion contained in the Old and New Testaments. The faith that Christians profess are called "creeds,", which in Latin are called "credo,' or 'symbols of faith.'

Such credo herein is the sum of broken parts presented as a token, a sign of recognition and communion between believers. It is a summary of the principle truths of faith serving as a fundamental point of reference for a Catechism; for the instruction of Christians, those seeking to know more about The Catholic way of life as a believer and an entry point for a non believer.

This book examines "the Credo" from the viewpoint of one man's indoctrination to the Church through his childhood, to his loss of faith in adult life, and a rekindling of belief through the symbols and signs and wisdom of age in an acknowledgement of a Higher Power. The belief in "The Credo " comes in the form of a search for the divine revelation of God, a personal communion with Him and a response of faith into spiritual action.

The Credo is examined as a sum of its parts described into various chapters of understanding for not only the benefit of the reader but the author of this book too. For it is by research and examination of the Catechism of Faith that this book has evolved to its ultimate conclusions.

For the Shepherds who care for their flock,
The flock who follow in faith,
And the lost sheep who are still searching.

"Our profession of faith begins with *God*, for God is the First and the Last, the beginning and the end of everything. The Credo begins with God the *Father*, for the Father is the first divine person of the Most Holy Trinity; our Creed begins with the creation of heaven and earth, for creation is the beginning and the foundation of all God's works."

- The Catechism of the Catholic Church.

Content:

Forward. 3

Introduction. 9.

Chapter 1. The Indoctrination. 13.

Chapter 2. Living the Credo 29.

Chapter 3. The Choice is always ours. 41.

Chapter 4. Symbols and Signs. 53.

Chapter 5. God's people and Prophetic Belief. 65.

Chapter 6. What do the renegades do? 75.

Chapter 7. Penance and Reconciliation. 83.

Chapter 8. The Sacrament of Matrimony. 95.

Chapter 9. Ancient Myths and Cultural Norms. 105.

Chapter 10. The Life in Christ. 123.

Chapter 11. The Vision of Belief. 135.

Chapter 12: The Credo. 143.

Catholic belief is succinctly expressed in the profession of faith or *credo* called the *Nicene Creed*:

I believe in one God,
the Father almighty,
maker of heaven and earth,
of all things visible and invisible.
I believe in one Lord Jesus Christ,
the Only Begotten Son of God,
born of the Father before all ages.
God from God, Light from Light,
true God from true God,
begotten, not made, consubstantial with the Father;
through him all things were made.
For us men and for our salvation
he came down from heaven,
and by the Holy Spirit was incarnate of the Virgin Mary,
and became a man.
For our sake he was crucified under Pontius Pilate,
he suffered death and was buried,
and rose again on the third day
in accordance with the Scriptures.
He ascended into heaven
and is seated at the right hand of the Father.
He will come again in glory
to judge the living and the dead
and his kingdom will have no end.
I believe in the Holy Spirit, the Lord, the giver of life,

who proceeds from the Father and the Son,

who with the Father and the Son is adored and glorified,

who has spoken through the prophets.

I believe in one, holy, catholic and apostolic Church.
I confess one Baptism for the forgiveness of sins and I look forward to the resurrection of the dead and the life of the world to come. Amen

INTRODUCTION

The solemn ritual of the sacrifice of the Mass in the Catholic Church of my childhood always began with an abridged version of the Gospel of John 1:1-18. In the beginning was the Word, and the Word was with God, and the Word was God. He was in the beginning with God. All things came to be through him, and without him nothing came to be. What came to be through him was life, and this life was the light of the human race; the light shines in the darkness, and the darkness has not overcome it.

The Mass was always in Latin back then for that was the language of the religion of the times. It always began and ended with the priest habitually kissing the altar to honour the sacrifice which represents Christ being the 'Sacrificial lamb' of God, where the miracle of the Eucharist occurs, for it has been a timely tradition. To this day the repeated process at the beginning and end of the Mass also symbolizes the bond between Christ and His Church, acknowledging also those martyrs, as relics of the furthering of the faith as an extension of peace and love to the church community. The Mass comes from the Latin 'Ite missa es' meaning 'to send out" as Jesus Christ sent his disciples out to the world to take his teachings to them.

The liturgy of the Mass in Latin seemed to have more of a heart rending spiritual essence to us children of the 1950s than it has today. Perhaps because in one's adult life the logical linear brain discerns more readily the practicability of symbols and signs of belief and spiritual practice than the mind of the innocence of childhood. The Latin Mass faded into the ether after Vatican 11, as did the Gospel of John 1:1-18 and the whole process opened up more to audience participation, when the priest faced the congregation instead of once having his back turned away from the the people towards the Tabernacle that housed the host of the body and the blood of Christ Eucharist for most of the celebration. Today as back then going to Mass is as much about spending time with God as it is with receiving the inner strength of spiritual grace by Christ's sacrificial act to live a Christian life. At the beginning the priest, accompanied by altar boy servers reaches the sanctuary, that part of the Church where the altar table is. He begins Mass by saying the sign of the cross; 'In the name of the Father, and of the Son and of the Holy Spirit, Amen.' This short prayer means that everyone is reminded that they are baptized into the One God in three persons, and so puts themselves into his protection. Then the congregation are given a few moments to reflect upon the things they have done or not done which offend others and God. The congregation is then invited to repent, or say sorry to God. This is because when believers repent for wrongdoing, God gives spiritual God grace for salvation.

The second part of Mass is called the 'Liturgy of the Word.' Liturgy is an ancient word, which came from the ancient Greeks meaning 'official work,' so Mass is part of the official prayer of the Church. In the liturgy of the Word, everyone listens to readings from the Bible; first, a story from the Old Testament which is completed by what Jesus Christ did, e.g. the story of the Israelites being fed on manna in the desert (Exodus chapter 16), is completed when Jesus Christ said 'I am the bread of life' (John chapter 6). Then a psalm is prayed or sung on the same theme. The second reading is usually a letter from St Paul and then everyone stands to listen to a reading from the Gospel, the story of Jesus. This reading will show how the Old Testament is completed by Jesus. After the readings everyone sits and listens to the homily, or sermon preached by the priest. To complete this part of the Mass, on Sundays, everyone recites the Credo, the statement of faith in God, and then an 'intercessions' that is, a set of prayers for local issues and people.

The third part of the Mass is called the liturgy of the Eucharist. 'Eucharist' means to give thanks, so it begins by the 'offertory' when we offer ourselves to God. This is symbolized by taking up the bread and wine which will become the Body and Blood of Jesus Christ. During the Eucharistic prayer everyone kneels to worship Jesus Christ who becomes present under the appearance of bread and wine when the priest says the 'consecration,' a sacred blessing believed to be by Christ, and whilst visible, nothing appears to have changed, the change is one of substance, of what it is, a reenactment of the last supper, when Jesus broke the bread, gave it to his disciples and said: "Take ye and eat of it, for this is my body.' Then he took the cup of wine and said: ``Take ye and drink this wine, for this is my blood." The priest then offers up the bread and wine proclaiming: "When we eat this bread and drink this cup, we proclaim your death O' Lord until you come in glory." Those who are able to receive 'Holy Communion' then process up to receive, either in one kind (just the host, the Body) or in two kinds (from the cup as well). Those unable to receive Holy Communion, either because they are not Catholics, or because as Catholics they have disobeyed a serious law of the Church and have not been reconciled to the Church, are invited to come forward and receive a blessing, which can be called a spiritual communion.

The final part of Mass, the concluding rite is quite short – after some time to reflect on the Eucharist (Holy Communion) everyone stands and the priest says a final short prayer, asking God for help to use the graces we have received in Mass to help us in our daily lives. He then blesses everyone in the name of the Father and the Son and the Holy Spirit, so we all leave knowing we have worshiped God, through the second person of the Trinity, of Father, Son and Holy Spirit and strengthened by him to live our lives in the world. To the priest's final words, 'The Mass is ended. Go in the peace of Christ, to love and serve the Lord,' the congregation replies. 'Thanks be to God.' Much has been written on the central mystery of the Eucharist and St. Cyril of Jerusalem writing in the late fourth century said, 'Do not look upon the bread and wine as something ordinary, for, by the Lord's own words, they are his Body and Blood. Even though perception suggests this to you, let faith grant you certainty. Do not judge the matter by taste! Be firmly convinced by faith that you have become worthy of the Body and Blood of Christ.'

So it was that the mystery of faith of my former years left me in my adulthood, for it no longer seemed to provide the necessary ingredient for living in this world. But tragic circumstances caused great calamity in my life. I tried to drink my way out of it, and ultimately collapsed into a state of mental, physical and spiritual exhaustion. I was like a drowning man desperately holding on to life grasping at straws. It was then I cried out for help and God answered in unexpected creative ways, but still I did not return to the faith. The slow work of God came through the steps of Alcoholics Anonymous. I entered into a new way of life as a non drinker, a believer in a Higher Power who I embraced as the manifested God of creativity. I handed over to whatever and wherever He led me. However, whilst I had concluded that my former Catholic belief related only to the logical linear, half brain approach to spirituality, I still carried the scaffolding of my former belief, and in time the desire to partake in the liturgy of the Church returned. For I began to miss the symbols and signs that guided my spirituality as a child. I came to believe that as the brain itself has a logical linear side essential to living in this world, it equally has a creative one. And it follows that the sum of both parts are necessary to the spiritual self health as are the physical and mental aspects of the other. So it seems a natural progression to put one's boat of personality on the spiritual waters of life, trim the sail and go with the flow in the belief that God guides one to the direction he so chooses. However, no action can be taken unless one has faith and the logical signs and symbols of Christianity seems now to be a wise move in the right direction of putting creativity pursuits into both the hand of God and the practical outcome in the world, even if one now believes in the process of living in this world but not being of it. Everything in life in this modern world is in a constant state of transformation and fluctuation, and the 'Yin' of the logical mind and the 'Yang' of the creative seem to be a way the coming together in measuring the for and against of the positive and negative aspects of one's spiritual progress or regression. By further examination, I began to conclude one may apply the Credo of Catholic belief to all aspects of daily living without prejudice to the belief in a manifested God of the creative. In fact both work hand in hand as I was coming to realize. But how to apply the understanding of all the principles of the Catholic religion of my upbringing to the everyday, to live a spiritual existence in the process without breaching the teachings of The Church. The 'Essence of Grace' imposed on us by God for our salvation, a gift provided by the sufferings and death of Christ on the cross.

How does a lost sheep return to the fold when Canon law and doctrines of Faith and moral in the Church teachings run counter to the reality of one's life in the now? It seems to be that the only way to marry the belief of Catholicism with my own soundness of mind, logic of it, was to appear directly to God, let Him not judge me but consider the faith of the body of his people which may include me in Mass and Eucharist celebration. So to achieve my mission of understanding and acceptance of a New Age religious Catholic belief of my logical mind and marry it all with my belief in a manifested Godhead, I needed to review my past indoctrination to the faith, examine my conscious to my understanding and belief in the faith and morals as historically laid down in Church teachings, and piece together a threat of hope in applying them to my life today. It is therefore that I use "The Credo" as the focal point to my quest in applying questions and answers to the mission. It is, as you dear reader shall discover, my journey back in time that draws this story to be of benefit,"The Credo" to daily living. It is for you to determine if I have achieved my mission herein. Now read on.

CHAPTER 1.

THE INDOCTRINATION

Father Cusack towered over us small boys like Cyclops, the one eyed giant of Greek mythology. We were seated six in all on a long bench, pigeons on a coop stick waiting in fear and awe for our first instruction into the Latin language of the Catholic Mass celebration. We, having been chosen, had reached what was considered the age of reason. A timely age of seven years to be indoctrinated into the ways of 'Catholic Faith' and servitude as Altar boys. The Godly Irish priest was in reality 5-foot-6 tall, with a ruddy face leathered from too much Australian sunshine, of stocky build; more like a boundary rider than a man of the cloth. He was to teach us rote style this foreign language and drum it into thick skulled boys more interested in running about wildly in the bush than after school hours corporal punishment of one who preached the word of God. The goodly friar was the turning point in our learning the black and white doctrine of the Church, the faith of our fathers's Holy faith in Latin. To his credit he got through to us without so much as a clout across our heads. For he had a better instrument of instruction than we encountered with the Sisters of (No) Mercy in our schooling. Fr. Cusack used as his weapon of "Mass Instruction," a ten foot long stock-whip which he wheeled wildly over our heads and cracked whenever any one of us misinterpreted the Latin lingo or mispronounced a word in his view. In point of fact he not only had a one eyed view of religious doctrine but he literally had only one eye.

The priest had lost his left eye back in Ireland at a football match. Apparently a woman in the crowd had lent back and her hat pin had penetrated his eye as he lent forward to observe an exciting happening on the field of play. The tragic event did not hamper his skill with a stock-whip though. On more than one occasion the sound of that stock-whip crack and the whistle of the wind overhead sometimes felt like I would shit my pants but I never did. It was in the nature of us children of the early 1950s to pay attention, accept physical punishment for our sins when administered, so as not to deprive us of divine grace. To be fair, it was more the nuns who inflicted physical pain with the cane during our primary education for it was a common threat of belief that 'to spare the rod was to spoil the child.' I took more beatings from those good Samaritans than ever I received from the Marists in my senior year of boarding school education. It was a matter of course, be that in class for not paying attention or a considered misdemeanour on the sporting field. Fr. Cusack in all the years we served him and learnt the ways of the Italian lingo in his Church liturgy teaching never once raised his hand to hit any of us boys. But when it came to that stock whip-well that was enough to put the fear of God into me and cower to the duties assigned. Even today when I hear a crack of thunder or a car backfire I find a Latin phrase passing my lips without so much as a mindful trigger.

  We boys served Mass on a round robin basis seven days a week. The duties included ensuring everything was in readiness for the Mass celebration. Ensuring the Nuns had laid out the priestly vestments for the Mass, the communion chalice, water and wine flasks full and on the altar at the ready for the priest communion and the administering of the Holy Eucharist to the congregation. Checking that the soft cloth for cleaning the sacred implements were at hand when the Mass had ended. Apart from dressing up in religious regalia, we servants bowed and scraped our way through the Latin replies of the Mass celebration, and rang a gong at the appropriate time when the priest faced the people with the body and blood of Christ. My duties changed the day I almost poisoned my Latin teacher. It was at the priest's communion when he ran out of wine after partaking of the host to wash the residue down. I was quickly sent off to the side storeroom to get more sacred altar wine. A re-corked well labeled bottle ensured me I had the necessary sacred Elixia, the wine of spiritual life. I poured the contents of the bottle into the flask on the altar and served the priest. Fr. Cusack almost died on the spot. I had administered an alcohol cleaning fluid to him which he downed in one gulp and his face colour changed a deathly white. From that day onward I was given other duties of a less hazardous kind. One of these was ringing the "Angelus" on the big bell tower that stood high on a pole high on the hill on the Church grounds. The Angelus Catholic devotion commemorating the Incarnation of Jesus, included the reciting of the Hail Mary said morning, noon and night, and the call to pray was noted by the sound of the Church bell.

  It was my daily duty to ring that bell which echoed across the local township calling Catholics to pause for a few moments in prayerful reflection. Like a heavenly messenger, the Angelus calls man to interrupt his daily, earthly routines and turn to thoughts of God, of the Blessed Mother, and of eternity. The manner of ringing the Angelus seems to have varied little since the beginning of the devotion.... Old monastic records, going back to the fifteenth century, show that the bell-ringer was directed, 'to toll the Ave-bell nine strokes at three times, keeping the space of one Pater, Our Father, and one Ave, Hail Mary, between each of the three tolling.' Like everything in my primary school education it became habitual and rote learning. The same repetitive learning methodology applied to the alphabet of additions, subtractions, multiplications and divisions, as it did to learning the difference between verbs, adverbs, nouns and adjectives. And of course this method was maintained in indoctrination of the belief in Christ birth, death, resurrection and ascension into heaven. Little was taught in those early years of God the Father, outside of the then Latin version of John's Revelation of the word in the celebration of the Mass and the Apostles creed.

The Good Samaritan's focused more on the Trinity of Father, Son and Holy Ghost with prime emphasis on Jesus the second person. On every work page of our school subjects exercise books we had to write 'JMJ' on the upper lefthand corner denoting the names of Jesus, Mary and Joseph. Then on the right I. O.G.D meaning in latin Omnibus Glorificetur Deus - all for the glory of God. Later in life I read it as an abbreviation for what had become a different indoctrination for me .i.e. I.O.G.D, I often get drunk. But that's another story for later in this book. Gradually the holy Sisters of (No) Mercy had us change that abbreviation to AMDG, Ad Majorem Dei Gloriam with an emphasis on obedience, faith, penance, and prayer so that God might be glorified ...Sometimes we learnt these lessons of indoctrination with patient explanation by our teachers and at other times, when the mood of a particular nun or two was weighed down by a dark cloud overhead, the sacrifice to Jesus for our defects of character was administered with much force and a good caning as a consequence. So it was no small wonder that I had built into my structural DNA a scaffold of the black and white nature of Catholicism by the time I headed off to boarding school and further indoctrination of a different kind. That of the French order of Marist Brothers who held the view that every boy in their care was of equal standing in the eyes of the Lord, and that equally their own sometimes warped view of heavy handedness in inflicting their will upon us innocent children was a must to our growing into men of substance. We were to stand for God with our school Motto:. The Latin - In Meliora Contende-to strive for better things. The Marist Brothers order recruited common men of rudimentary ability to educate young boys teaching them to be independent, strong, brave committed to rise above mediocrity with noble vision, to appreciate the things that are worthwhile, to choose what is right, despise the petty, shun all selfishness, be pure and happy, docile yet courageous, devoting everything to God above all things. The one bright note in all of that was great acceptance and fellowship of boys and old boys alike. Whilst there were elite snobs who came from privileged classes that school was a great leveller. We all learnt to see each other as being no better or no worse than the next person. Joey's to this day is a member of the GPS school system based on British Elite school principles. The Marist brothers however would have none of that! We were privileged to have the education we got and a lifetime of friendship and assistance no matter what station in life we held in the future. Of course I didn't buy it all and knew that in the real world there is a pecking order and thus I weaved my way through the College education system and survived to tell this tale.

It would be remiss of me not to explain a little about the Brotherhood of Marist and its founder to give you the reader and insight into the philosophy to which I was educated.The Founding Father of the Order, Marcellin Champagnat was born in Marlhes, France in 1789 and died 51 years later in 1840 at a place called Our Lady of the Hermitage, in the valley of Gier about thirty kilometres from the place of his birth. He trained and worked as a parish priest and Founder in this region throughout his lifetime. He never did anything that usually accompanies greatness, he had no credentials but himself. He lived in a region of materially poor, educationally ignorant and of moral low ebb: for the French Revolution and Napoleonic Wars had taken its toll on all of such districts in France at the time. Marcellin, with great opposition, founded an Order of Brothers intent on alleviating the misery of the poor and needy for both near and far flung places. The authorities considered him mad, incapable of such work, lacking sufficient brains and destitute of sufficient resources. But when he died in 1840, some 320 or so men had already chosen to follow his lead. Within 20 years this number had expanded to over 2000 men, so that today there are more than 7000 Brothers teaching over 500,000 students throughout the world.

For the Australian Marist and particularly St. Joseph's College the link with the Founders spirit has been quite close. Br. Francois, who was the Order's first Superior-General and a close personal friend of the founder died as late as 1881, the year in which St.Joseph's College was founded. So we realize that the Brothers who came here from Europe had carved the College Chapel, living quarters and first class rooms by hand from the sandstones of Woolwich Point, in the late 19th century. Many of Champagne's first Brothers, who personally had known him for his spirit and charisma, applied his methodology from the day the first stone was laid at Joeys. We boys who were educated by his design for living, be that by a more modern template of the founder, followed the characteristics of his simplistic indoctrination from the very first lesson. We learnt early to have no pretence, learnt to show compassion to the less fortunate, to be open minded, to have a devotion to the Virgin Mary and to trust in God. The attitude of gratitude was instilled in us, to learn to never give up despite what life may dish out. That despite disappointment we can fight on, stick to all things, don't lie down. We had to study hard and train hard no matter what we were attempting. If we make a mistake and when we're in trouble, we can get over it, not give up, bear no grudges, and strive on. This is what Champagne taught and this is how he lived and how the Marist who taught us tried to instil.

My bedroom so to speak was a dormitory full of boys mainly from the country but some even from overseas. We outnumbered the city boys four to one. I thanked God for that as most of them were little shits. The dormitory consisted of wire frame base beds much like you see on country fence gates. The bed had a steel framed head with cross bar which was an ideal place to hang one's towel after showering or to dry sports socks and football gear. They were the only items we had to wash, the rest of our dirty clothes were placed in our personal laundry bag which had name and laundry number sown on the bag. All our clothing had that number and mine coincidentally was the same number as Uncle Dick's shop number in George Street city opposite the Central railway. Over the five years I lived in that building the dormitories varied from ones which had worn out old mattresses to ones near the roof which leaked like a sieve above my bed. I had to move the bed aside and place buckets around in order to stay dry in bed and not slip on the wet timber floor when going to the toilet in the dark of the midnight hour.

The regimented lifestyle of lights out in the dormitory by nine thirty in the evening and into bed, rise to the clap of a Marist hand at six, make the bed and take a quick shower, be dressing for Mass at seven, breakfast at eight, and into class at nine until twelve noon followed by lunch was daily routine ingrained in the brain and like robots we went about the place without question. There was a break for an hour to relax over a meal and catch up with friends then back to school work until three in the afternoon. Sport always loomed high on the agenda from three thirty until five thirty, then it was an evening meal at six and back to study at seven until nine in the evening. It was straight to the dormitory after that to hand wash sports gear and socks. Fortunately metal cross bars at bedhead were ideal clothes lines. Sometimes one or two boys would have a challenge as to how long they could wear their dirty socks without washing them. It was their policy to hang the socks at the end of their bed at night like they had been washed and the stink soon got objections from the masses of boys calling for them to yield their filthy game challenge. Ultimately the resident brother in charge of the dormitory would force them to wash or cane them into submission. It was the only time I was in agreement with the brothers on the matter of 'sparing the rod and spoiling the child.' On Fridays and weekends the routine changed somewhat. Friday was military cadets day, so we dressed in military uniform and were required to clean and polish our boots, whiten our webbing and gators and look the part throughout the day. After school we put on our military hats and supposedly assumed a military mental attitude for the rest of the day, until meal time. This involved marching to the beat of a routine, like troops who were being prepared for some future battle. We troops had to stand to attention for hours on end, learn the drill of slope arms, stand at ease and stand easy.

A General salute was also a matter of course for pending passing out parades where the Governor General would turn up at our 'military day' inspect the troops and make a long and boring speech. The boring speech that followed usually resulted with two or more cadets passing out on parade from heat exhaustion whilst suffering the verbose onslaught. The idea of doing our Cadet Apprenticeship never appealed to me from the first time I donned a military uniform. My maverick spirit just could not accept the brand that we were meant to live by during those cadet days. I guess I was somewhat of a conscientious objector before I ever had heard the phrase. The idea that fellow classmates who were normally good blokes could become right bastards just because they wore an officer's uniform I always revolted against. This usually resulted in being singled out for special punishment as a consequence. The punishment I took on as a matter of discipline was of a 'non military style' for which I accepted with an attitude of gratitude and which baffled the sadist who inflicted it. What he and his superior 'militant' brother considered formally legitimate I used to my advantage. The punishment was to shock one into the reality that one had to knuckle down and buckle up, be a team player so that if the occasion arose and someone somewhere knowingly or unknown started a future war, we with military indoctrination would be on the ready and maybe survive the onslaught. At any rate this wayward cadet was always punished for minor mistakes of which I always felt sure the mastermind always had a personal agenda to inflict pain. He could not do this during the normal routine of school life, except maybe on the Rugby field without a good canning for his ghastly deeds.

My punishment usually consisted of a drill; like being loaded with a dozen 303 rifles across my arms and being made to duck walk back and forth across a football oval. This punishment I accepted as a great way to strengthen my back and legs for the coming football season. The weight on my arms proved effective in flick passing the ball in a Rugby match. The ball seemed to feel as light as a feather after my military fitness punishment. Whilst I did not have the outward appearance of muscle growth, I had gained extra strength from the punishment. The other more common punishment was to stand at attention holding my rifle by the barrel at arms length without flinching or moving in any way. The punishment normally lasted about three minutes if you could keep the rifle still. Nine times out of ten, the arm would go into a pain spasm and the rifle would move just enough to have to repeat the drill process all over again. The better part of the Cadet life was going off to a military base for two weeks to learn the ropes from the military in a military atmosphere. We did many long route marches in the middle of the night, ran through jungle like conditions with rifles always at the ready.

Whilst our school had a rifle range to practice on, we had more opportunities with live ammunition at the base. Part of our experience also included being tied in like cargo on Hercules aircraft and taken on test flights and climbing all over fighter aircraft in the hangars after being given the privilege of watching the air acrobatic team put on a show. We usually traveled by train to military camps, which was a time for unraveling a toilet roll or two, holding one end and letting the bulk of the roll go out the window of the speeding train. The new Master of Discipline happened to be on the last leg of our speeding train on one occasion . He was stationed two carriages back and when I let go of the roll out the window it was perfect timing. The C.E.O. Marist, Master of Discipline, just happened to stick his head out the window at that precise moment to cop the full force of the toilet roll in the face. I quickly shot my head back in the carriage and escaped without recognition. He did come looking for the culprit but I looked innocently at him as if I knew nothing about it. Otherwise it would have been six of the best on each hand with his cane on my return back to school after holidays.

The RAAF Base was at Queanbeyan on the New South Wales side of the border near Canberra, the training location for the Sabre Jet Fighter Squadron as well as the troop carrying Hercules aircraft. We had the experience of taking a jet flight and experiencing the pull of gravity on the body riding in a non pressurised aircraft. Our routine at the Base, when not assisting in the cleaning of aircraft and our .303 rifles and equipment was military drills, long route marches around the base and getting to know and understand the routine of air force personnel. The best part of the military base was the food. After living in a boarding school and eating what was back then very basic, the food the soldiers ate in their refectories was to us five stars. It was a real pleasure to eat like half starved refugees at a banquet. Breakfast, lunch and dinner was always a treat and you could go back as many times as you liked for more. It was better than my Mum's home cooking, as back then the family Sunday lunch was the best meal of the week which usually consists of three basic vegetables and a lamb roast with gravy, baked chicken or an occasional roast duck.

A resident priest in full military uniform said the morning Mass on Sunday, so any boy who volunteered to attend that Mass and take communion was awarded a sleep-in and late breakfast with the fighter squadron. I jumped at that opportunity as it meant missing a routine foot march around the base carried out in the middle of the night fully equipped with a pack and rifle. I never saw any sense in that but a sadistic NCO thought otherwise. Once the majority of the boys went off on their drill, a mate and myself who had time to kill before Sunday Mass headed for the shower recess and proceeded to block the drainage system and turned on all the showers, getting great delight flooding the place out. Thinking back, we were just two little bored shits. I never bothered to confess that to the priest that morning, piously attending Mass and then running to the Mess for the banquet breakfast brunch with the Jet Fighter Squadron. A fellow classmate and I were the same two cadets later reported as attempting to cross the Queanbeyan river Weir against the force of the stream overflow. We both made it to the middle of the torrent of water, but got swept over the edge of the Weir and downstream at the rate of knots. Fortunately a branch protruding into the river was the lifesaver and I made it to the river bank to find my friend lying there exhausted from the experience. We made it back to Base as undetected half drowned rats. Thankfully there was no roll call in our absence. We were later singled out for KP- kitchen duty, being under suspicion of being up to something. Whilst the rest of the Cadet troops were attending to their uniforms for the next parade we scored kitchen working gear that were military issue. I had to roll up the legs and sleeves to wear mine. They were tagged 'EL' meaning extra large when I should have had an 'S' for small size. The only consolation was they hung down a long way in the crutch as it gave me the mistaken impression that I had a new status among my contemporaries as a 'long dick.'

Our Air Force Cadets unit attended that camp but never once fired a rifle. That did come later at our school rifle range and at future camps. Between study of aircraft recognition (plane spotting) in the unlikely event that an enemy aircraft attempted to invade our school.

However back at Joeys we did get to mess around a bit with military weaponry. A group of us cadets under a junior officers supervision managed to get mortar duty which included firing a dummy bomb.. Our practice session was on the same oval at the back of the school where I had my past corporal punishments inflicted. We set the sights of the mortar on the intended target, a drum near the furthest boundary fence. The oval being raised above a side street with a line of colonial houses along its perimeter We had a greater chance of hitting the target or at worst the fence behind it. The fence was made largely of blocks of sandstone which could take the impact of an A-Bomb, so we figured if we missed the target we would not do to much damage to the fence with a blank mortar shell. Due to the weight of the projectile encased in steel, one cadet had the duty of holding the mortar gun whilst the others duty was to set the fire in the hole so to speak. We were pretty confident but just to make sure we set the target range a hundred meters higher than the target. Our intention was for the bomb to rocket upwards instead of outward and try to hit the target with a downward motion. The supervisor knew little about mortars and we knew nothing! On ignition the rocket bomb flew up and away over the fence and appeared to be heading for the house opposite. The woman of the house had taken her young children out to play on the front lawn precisely at the time the bomb headed downward from the sky above. It buried deep into the front lawn a couple of centimetre from the two children. Watching that bomb hurtling down towards those kids seemed like an eternity. We rescued the bomb unnoticed by the mother and quickly returned the mortar to our armoury. In our setting mortar sights we failed to allow for the fact that the oval height had been raised 20 meters with top soil when being prepared for football season.

I was indoctrinated into the summer rowing season in my first term at Joeys as a Coxswain. Our rowing shed was an old timber building that housed five rowing shells and our only speed boat. We had a full time caretaker who lived like a hermit in a wooden cottage next door to the shed. Bernie was a part of the place, nature's gentleman and an alcoholic. The brothers and the boys felt sorry for him and he was always treated with respect. His job was to ensure everything was in place in and outside the shed when we all vacated the premises. The old school tidal pool was behind Bernie's cottage and next door to the main shed. It was always full of green slime but it didn't seem to bother us much, we just swam through it for a length or two and headed for a cold shower over a dirty old bathtub on the floor above the pool. It was almost winter as we ritually lined up for the cold shower when Brother BJ appeared at the entry. Two senior boys had, unknown to the rest of us, taken the speed boat for a midnight spin on some wild escapade, returning it to the boat shed before dawn. They were both young senior 18 year old boys, strong and fit and were drying themselves off as BJ approached.

We were all told to stand in our own nakedness along the shed wall parameter. I remember Peach was still standing ringing wet when BJ bellowed and eyeballed each one of us. Peach turned off the shower and stood ice cold still as did the rest of the rowing team in that room. He still had a semi erection and I admired its size, making a mental note to masturbate more often in the hope that I could develop one similar. Peach's erection soon subsided when JB commenced his punishment on those two strong lads. He caned them over and over until their bodies began to convulse. Eyes cast down afraid to look up, we all stood in fear that we would be next. Both boys didn't cry but their bodies were acting independently of their head. They both admitted that they had taken the speed boat for a spin. BJ recommenced his punishment, and both lads were a complete mess. BJ only stopped thrashing them when he got far too exhausted to continue. The Brother's eyes were wild and his mouth seemed to shape into a kind of sneer, drooling saliva like Lawrence of Arabia when he slaughtered the retreating Turks. BJ was a strong man who could bring down that stick so hard that it would seem like the pain would never end. The memory of that punishment is ingrained in my memory bank forever. When Irishmen are crazy they are really crazy. I only copped it once from BJ, apart from a back-hand over the head with a close knuckle fist. He gave me a canning across my buttocks for talking after night study on another occasion. It was nothing like those two rowers copped but it was painful enough. Later our illustrious Br. Headmaster limited BJ's action with the use of the cane when he had broken a student's wrist in his application to inflict more pain. The Headmaster was a bit like calling the pot black, he too wielded the cane with great power but he was not a patch on BJ's unique ability and possibly sexually frustrated actions of extreme cruelty.

In my time at school rowing was considered a summer sport and the then Headmaster didn't much like boys leaving school grounds to attend training and rowing in weekend regattas. He had the view that he could keep an eagle eye on the 'prisoners' within the school bounds much better than second hand reports from outside the school. In part he was right because the manyof us got up to a lot of mischief which required much discipline. That Headmaster had a mean streak when it came to rowers. When I coxed the eight in 61, we were on the water by 5.30.am. each day for training sessions. It meant that if BJ had us out on the water longer than usual then it was a very quick cold shower, dressed in school gear and a run up the hill to make the 7 am Mass with the rest of the school.

 As Cox I had the additional duties of washing down the boat as it came off the water, drying it off with a cloth and applying graphite on the leather binds, where the oar met the rollick, so all the oars were at the ready for the next training session in the afternoon. On this occasion we all had to move in double quick time and despite our best effort arrived at the schools after Mass had started. The crew elected to hide in the downstairs toilet area rather than draw attention to our late arrival. I consider it best to run to the Chapel on the first floor entry being only five minutes late. As I passed the Headmaster's office he was standing at the door and he called me back and questioned the reason for my lateness. He had me kneel and gave me six of the best on each hand to ensure there would never be a repeat of that performance. I managed to make it a habit to be late just to spite him and always got past his door without further detection.

 My claim to fame as a country boy was as a 'North Coaster.' There were a number of us who traveled too and from school at the beginning and end of each term on the North Coast mail. A lot of our clan came from the Hastings district. We rode the second class carriages which were divided into opposing bench railway green tanned leather seats wide enough to hold four boys bums with some latitude for spreading out. Above each seat was a wire rack for luggage and on the dark wooden walls hung old photos of bush scenes depicting railway activity or the unveiling of a new train. Each compartment had a metal foot warmer which was great in the winter when the floor would get ice cold. Placing one's socked feet on the gas filled metal cylinder guaranteed warmth and the residue of chilblains in the not too distant future. We also had a large container of water and a glass on a shelf attached to one wall just in case an urge to drink might overtake us. I can't remember any of us ever drinking that water. We preferred to buy a tea bag and hot water with some 'railway biscuits' at major stopping points along the way. It gave us enough time to stretch our legs, go to the platform toilet and get some fresh air away from the soot spewing from the coal fired engines that pulled the train to its next destination.

The journey from Central station took about twelve hours to my hometown platform. Most of my fellow intrepid travellers had alighted by the time the train reached Taree. Heading home on the night train was always an adventure. We didn't sleep much and would close the sliding carriage doors and bind the door handles with school ties so as not to be disturbed by the night guard. Once he had punched our ticket we were pretty much left to our own devices. That is unless there was a complaint from another nearby passenger or we got up to some mischief. As a delaying tactic we used our school ties to secure the double handled doors, so if the guard appeared and tried to open the double carriage doors, they appeared to be stuck. Securing the doors like that gave us time to dispense with our cigarettes out the window and clear the smoke before undoing the doors. Our exploits, apart from smoking and the odd drink on our journey homeward, included playing 'spot what tree is that' for each power pole we passed. The idea was to pick a tree type and see how many poles were made from that tree over an allotted distance along the side of the track. Each power pole had an identification stamp denoting its tree source. TT was tallow wood, PP was pinewood, GG was grey gum and so on. This amused us long enough until we got bored and then we would come up with a song or two and sing along until the wee small hours. The train snaked its way north where at each major stop the majority of Joey's rabble jumped off at Newcastle. We always lost one or two around Foster with most of the clan alighting at Taree.

I recall one year returning from school at the end of the term, we shared a compartment with five other boys. Somebody asked for a drink of water and a friend Chris reached up and grabbed the bottle and glass and just as he was about to pour it, quick as a flash he threw the bottle out the window. As luck would have it the train was passing a railway siding at that precise moment and the bottle shattered all over the concrete platform. The Guard in the next carriage happened to be leaning out the window at the time and caught the action. Chris grabbed his suitcase and quickly made his way up the train into the next carriage with the train guard hot on his tail. Chris was due to alight at the next station so before the guard could grab him, opened the carriage door and jumped from the moving train. The suitcase burst open on the platform with all his worldly possessions flying everywhere and Chris rolling over and over on the platform. The last sighting of Chris was when he left the platform running with clothes sticking out of that suitcase, he never did return to Joey's at the start of the next term. Another friend David and I were the last to leave the train heading north. We made a pact to return back to school the morning before we were due back. We caught the night train arriving in Central at dawn. We had a game plan and the day's activities in the city worked out well in advance. Making our way by bus to the College, we first checked out from a list on the notice board our allotted dormitories for the next term. The idea was that we would firstly test each bed to find the most comfortable. Next we helped each other to pick the best location in the Dormitory. It was simply a matter of moving the best sprung wire bed frame and mattress near a window with a view and doing a swap. This was closely followed by unpacking our bags in our lockers, taking a shower and getting dressed into some casual gear to catch a bus back to the city.

 We would start the day with a big breakfast followed by a morning film show. After the movie, we usually made our way to the State theatre for ice-cream and popcorn whilst we watched the latest newsreels. The State film clips ran on a non stop basis, so you could enter the theatre at any time and watch until the same news came around for the second time. It was then off to buy a newspaper to see what other films were on that we could watch. By the end of the day we returned back to school to greet our fellow inmates and catch up on holiday stories. I always went to bed after that day of activity with a roaring headache and flakiness. This mad movie day activity continued for the rest of our time at Joey's together.

 David had great difficulty settling into one particular class. It was a personality class with the Br. Jack of all Trades.. He taught us mathematics for our leaving year and was also a rowing coach so I had a bit to do with him outside class. David, on the other hand, had a fall out and Br. Jack refused to teach him but allowed him to attend his class. By the time mid year came around we had a pile of homework to do each night. Math, English, Modern History, Ancient History, Geography and Economics, if you weren't studying a language but it always left us with overload for evening homework. Our class had a meeting one evening and we all mutually agreed that we would skip doing our Math's homework to fit in all the rest of our assignments for the next day's assessments. When Br. Jack of all Trades asked a couple of us to answer questions relating to the previous night's assignment, the retort was "We didn't do it Brother." Br. Jack then requested those of us who hadn't done our homework to stand up. The whole class except my friend David got to their feet. Jack, taking the metal edge of his ruler, began systematically to crack each of us over the knuckles for our failure to adhere to his orders. When he came to David, he was still seated. Br. Jack asked him if he had completed his homework. David's answer duplicating ours and Br. Jack ordered him to stand and take his punishment. He replied that he was not in the goodly brother's class anymore so couldn't be punished. Br. Jack replied: "You are now back" and proceeded to bash him across the knuckles too. Both David and I failed mathematics in the Leaving Certificate. The mathematics paper had changed to a two hour examination with the first 32 questions being multiple choice. It took me 30 minutes to complete the multiple choice and I left the exam room not bothering to do the rest of the paper. As it happened I scored 32 % for the paper. So if I had stayed and attempted the whole thing I may well have managed a pass. The strange nature of career events throughout my lifetime have always been mathematically centred. I pursued a banking career, work in engineering which involved mathematical statistics, worked with actuaries in insurance and later ran my own businesses all interrelated with mathematics. In David's case, he drew a perfect replica of a D9 bulldozer for the mathematics examination and had he been marked on that drawing he would have scored 100%. David in his career at one stage owned nine D9 bulldozers which he used to employ drivers to cut through the jungles of New Guinea to open up new territories for both the NG Government and private enterprise there. Both David, and another friend Leonard who did not complete his Leaving certificate, used their timber career talents in volunteering to complete unpaid tasks for the Catholic Church. David built a timber church at Ulong out of his own pocket and Leonard a new Catholic primary school at Walcha. The indoctrination of the Marist was well founded in those two men's hearts.

  I was pretty good at chemical formula and was not too bad in Maths algebra, but of the rest of Math and Science I just didn't have the head. I used to get in the high 80s for Chemistry and 30s in Science. So naturally when I got to L.C. year I switched to Economics which was the first year it was introduced as a Leaving Certificate subject. I was still not applying myself too well in class, preferring to skip Economics and Ancient History classes in favour of disappearing to the library to read about historic adventurers. If and when I got caught I gave the impression that I was busy in study. To be fair our Economics and Ancient history master was one and the same person but not not the best teacher. We called him Colossus because of his sizeable tales of historic sexual exploits of known leaders we studied. Brother's name gradually change to "Spunky,' the nickname back then of someone who spoke frequently of penis complex and erections. My marks in geography were of A grade standard having topped the class in the half yearly trials. This already assured me of 10 marks in the final paper. My Modern History papers were used by the teacher for honours students research so I had no problem in that quarter. Wool classing was still a Leaving Certificate final subject as was music. They were the last two examinations before the Ancient History exam eleven days later. So I read the whole syllabus within the 11 days, concocted some algebraic formula mixed with history dates and got myself a pass.

In conclusion, we were taught at school to live by the 'Golden rule' of doing unto others and be compassionate, independent and free. The lessons therein took more than my school years to learn that rule and that life is not about Doug at all. My holidays ended abruptly as Dad insisted on employing me until my Leaving Certificate results came out in the press. I did not enjoy working in the garage doing menial tasks and returning home at night looking like I had fallen into a vat of grease. I was relieved to receive my results closely followed by a letter from the Commonwealth Bank congratulating me on my results and offering me a start at the local branch for two pounds above the basic wage of a bank officer. The exam results ensured I would be accepted for the next intake for Teachers College if I so wished to pursue that option.

Through all my early education, religion played an important part in shaping my character, be that flawed by defects and lack of consciousness when under the influence of alcohol. For I was a dyed in the wool alcoholic who knew no boundaries when affected by the drink. I didn't know I was an alcoholic back then. Frequent confession played an important part in me overlooking my waywardness. For in times of regretful behaviour and shame, I figured that wiping the soul slate clean from the hangover of the night before was a justifiable means of continuing on the road to success and the moral of my logical linear belief and upbringing in the Catholic Church ensured that God understood where others didn't. Time and tide would see me rise to great heights in the material world, working hard to provide for my family and become moderately rich. However, life has a way of testing one's will to endure and fate played a cruel turn on me. For a long time I let God and my indoctrinated teachings of my childhood go, when all that I believed in and lived by turned to dust.

28
 It would take a series of tragic events that came to pass in my adult life, resulting calamities that I could not find a way out off, a collapse into deep depression and long stints in rehabilitation before I found that I was powerless over alcohol and in a cry for help I turned to a God of my new understanding which proved to be a manifestation of my creative mind and not the logical linear one of my prior indoctrinated belief.

CHAPTER 2.

THE LIVING OF THE CREDO

God works in strange ways and I learnt to trust in his slow work on me as a sober alcoholic. It was then, and only then, I came to believe in not only the manifested risen Christ of my creative brain, but in time I was drawn back to the scaffolding of the symbolism and signs that I was educated to. The right brain thinking of a logical linear education and indoctrination of those goodly nuns and brothers, who despite making us suffer painful experiences all in the name of a loving Saviour, somehow infused a belief in religious rightfulness and that in my youth ultimately sunk in. The Nuns achieved the subliminal belief system in us children and the Brothers taught teenagers in theology. Between the two, I now consider fair grounding for the way of stewardship that in an adult lifetime one needs to know and put into practice. It has as far as I have come to believe caused me no permanent scars. Besides, it was not long after WW11 when I was grounded in the faith and was mindful of those who died and those poor souls who returned as scared shattered men as consequence. The religious nuns could obviously justify their actions in the light of the times. Equally the brothers of the late 1950s and early 1960s had cause to indoctrinate us young men with a moral code to live by in facing a real world of corruption and dastardly deeds that followed.

Whilst over the past two decades I had rejected the Church doctrines and logical belief of God in favour of the manifested one of my creative mind, I found my then belief fulfilled my spiritual self. I learnt to just hand over without definition to God, without a Church or religious Canon law to justify it. Many miraculous things happened to me to justify that I was on the right track. Of course, the acceptance of handing over to a power greater than self as in the AA third step had a lot to do with that. Whilst Step 3 is not meant to be a religious obligation, it nevertheless worked for me in that way. Quite possibly because of my former teachings of Church doctrine, that no longer appeared to work for me, as the Catholic God did not answer my prayers in my time of need , or so it seemed. The 3rd Step prayer was a notable exception, for not only did God answer my prayer, but it opened up for me a plethora of creative output, sending me on a new and productive course that was unexpected. So for what it is worth to you dear reader, here is that prayer; "God, I offer myself to Thee - to build with me and to do with me as Thou will. Relieve me of the bondage of self, that I may better do Thy will. Take away my difficulties, that victory over them may bear witness to those I would help with Thy Power, Thy Love, and Thy Way of life. May I do your will always!"

The very idea of just utilizing one's creative brain in a manifested belief is by man's very nature a lopsided viewpoint, or belief system. Particularly when one comes to prayer and meditation and going about living the way of sobriety in this world. I soon came to realize that whilst I sought to live in the world but not of it, one could not live with balance in the creative mind without embracing the logical brain. Man, like everything in nature is like a two sided coin, a double edged sword, or a plus and minus force field. By way of example no arrow, bullet or in today's world nuclear weapon can hit its target without opposing forces to guide it. God, I was coming to realize is the middle road between the logical brain and the creative manifestation. It is the void of nothingness where we find the balance of him, in existence of our spiritual likeness. He (by my former teachings) is the Alpha and the Omega, the beginning and end that encompasses everything, The desire for him is written into our hearts, because we are born to be in his image and likeness. Vatican 11 (1962-64) summed up the " I believe" as confessed in the Credo and celebrated in Church faith. Only in God can we find truth and happiness and he never stops searching for the dignity of man resting in that fact. We are called to communion with God. Invited to converse with God from the very moment of our being. For if Man is in existence, it is by that very nature that God created him though love, and it is thought by love that he continues to hold him in that existence. Man cannot live fully in accord with that truth unless he freely acknowledges that love and entrusts himself to his creator. And yet it is but by desire that one believes in God and it cannot be proven that he exists, and therein lies the mystery of it all.

In my final year of High school I was given a task to write a thesis in our religious theological examination. The question posed was at the beginning of life on earth what shows the awesome power of God, the story of God creating all in seven days, creating Adam in the Garden of Eden then Eve from his hip bone as his companion. Or was it the slow work of evolution where man (Adam) came from the Ape? My thesis first went along the lines of the book of Genesis in the Bible. Where God created all in seven days or did he create it as a long slow evolutionary process, eventually allowing man to come into entitlement of being from the Ape. Or did it all evolve from the Big Bang theory? Well the point of the reference in the question was proof of the 'power of God', and I went on to postulate that whatever viewpoint one might take, each in their own right proved the awesome power of God. But what of proof of God's existence, and for that matter the existence of Christ on earth, and his sacrificial act of dying on the cross to save mankind from his sinfulness?

Well, even Jorge Mario Bergogolio has his doubts in this regard. We now know him as Pope Francis, the Vicar of Christ on earth. At the time of his early studies for the priesthood Jorge had been working in a chemistry lab; under the tutelage of Esther Ballertino, a Science lecturer, and biochemist. Esther was an early influence. She mentored Bergoglio during his studies for his Science degree. They debated often on belief and unbelief in God and he had much love and great respect for her. She was later killed during the Dirty Wars in Argentina when assisting a nun who helped the poor people of the street at the time when the city was under siege from dangerous criminals. The young priest Jorge Bergogolio officiated at her funeral service and buried her remains in a Catholic cemetery despite her being an atheist throughout her life .

The personal and professional boy from Flores became a priest and his man of the world attitude finally melded into one with the voice of the famed Saint Ignatius. The teachings, writing and actions of St Ignatius of Loyola, Spanish priest and theologian, were the foundation stones of the apostolic order of the Society of Jesus in 1534. He was arguably the most influential figure in the Counter-Reformation of Catholicism. The Order, known for its missionary, educational, and charitable works, was a leading force in the modernizing of the Catholic Church. Ignatius was strongly influenced by the Renaissance and wanted Jesuits to be able to offer whatever ministries were most needed at any given moment, and especially, to be ready to respond to missions (assignments) from the Pope. Formation for priesthood normally takes between 8 and 17 years, depending on the man's background and previous education, and final vows are taken in service to all. Values commonly found in Ignatian spirituality are core values of the Gospel, such as authenticity, integrity, courage, love, forgiveness, hope, healing, service and justice. Several years after that, making Jesuit formations among the longest of any of the religious orders. Well Jorge Mario Bergogolio became one, part and parcel with the philosophy and actions of the Order, but he too was (is) a man of doubt when it comes to the Credo of the Catholic faith. Jorge wrote a document just prior to his ordination, which he called his creed.

"**I want** to believe in God the Father, who loves me like a son and in Jesus the Lord, who infused my life with His Spirit, to make me smile and, in so doing, lead me to the eternal Kingdom of Life.
I believe in the Church.
I believe in history that was pierced by the gaze of love of God. who, on the Spring day of September 21, came to meet me and invite me to follow Him.
I believe in pain, made fruitless by selfishness, in which I seek refuge.
I believe in the singiness of my soul that seeks to take without giving.
I believe that others are good and that I must love them without fear and without ever betraying them, never seeking my own security.
I believe in religious life.
I believe I want to love a lot.
I believe in the daily burning death from which I flee, but which smiles at me and invites me to accept her.
I believe in God's patience, welcoming, good, like a summer's evening.
I believe that my father is in Heaven, next to the Lord.
I believe that father Duarte is also there, interceding for my priesthood.
I believe in Mary, my Mother, who loves and will never leave me alone.
And I look forward to the surprise of everyday life in which love, strength, betrayal, and sin will always accompany me until the final meeting with that marvellous face, whose countenance I do not know, a face that I continually escape from but that I want to know and love. Amen"

In this man's creed there is a warm feeling of comfort and hope, yet some sadness and pain, a general concept of plea for sinners and no personal acknowledgment of specific wrong doing. His vision is being loved by God in a childlike way with the infusion of a Holy Spirit in one's life and ultimately eternal life. But we are brought down to earth with his admission of selfishness, stinginess, and his admission of taking without giving before once more turning to love and faith. His realistic poetic fleeing from 'daily burning death and its smiles of invitation to accept her, is an insight of the man's astounding knowledge of the will of the flesh in himself, as indeed it is in all of us. So could it be that I should take this credo for a Catholic logical renewal belief or write my own?

A Credo like Pope Francis can only be written and practiced when one has some firm commitment to the faith and a logical Catholic mission of love and service. Stewardship if you will to Christ like service to those less fortunate or suffering souls that befits the religious and can be applied in a simplistic way to those who practice the faith. Applying values of authenticity, integrity, courage, love, forgiveness, service and justice, as the Jesuits seemingly practice and the Pope advocates, and the faithful practice. Is no easy way of life. To live the logic of a Credo mission statement and apply it to a loving belief in a Creator God is one thing when that belief is embedded in the subconscious and is carried out with love consciously. What of one like me who has a belief in the conscious creative mind of a God of my own understanding; a manifestation of a Risen Christ, be he real or imaginary. Is it possible for me to rekindle the spirit of a belief in the Trinity, practice what I might preach in a belief in the Credo of the Catholic Church and live the Steps of Alcoholics Anonymous in unison? Well firstly, I needed to hone my will to the right brain logical belief of the Trinity, as well as continue the path of the manifested one of my creative imagination before I could embrace the Catholic credo or write a new one for myself. I figured that the God of my logical understanding could not be defined by the Bible nor any other text without further examination. God is without a doubt an Infinite Intelligence, a force that gives order and origin to everything in the entire universe. It is the prime source, the first cause of everything that comes into existence. Furthermore, we are defined as made in His image and likeness, if one is to believe so, are precise expressions of this force. As such, you have no limitations except those accepted or deliberately set up in your own mind. Additionally, all that is needed to access this creative power is absolute belief, total applied faith, and unwavering persistence. *Infinite Intelligence* is a neutral term that applies to all faiths. Buddhist, Christian, Hindu, Muslim, Jew, and practitioners of all world religions have names for this deity. Infinite Intelligence is a designation that can be adopted and understood by all. For the sake of this exercise I prefer to call Him the Creator God. However, the use of the Infinite Intelligence definition allows one to live in accord with a specifically defined purpose.

To achieve what I set your mind to requires two things. First is the acknowledgment that Infinite Intelligence is the prime source, the first cause of everything that comes into existence. This includes me. Without that knowledge I am unable to believe in my own unrestrained capacity for creative thought and action. If I don't believe in my inherent connection and oneness with the prime source, why would I believe in an unrestrained co-creative capacity? By contrast, if I do have this belief it becomes impossible to accept the constraint of my own abilities. To do so is the same as believing that the omniscient, omnipotent, everlasting being of Infinite Intelligence has its own limitations. Second is daily self affirmation or prayer of my life purpose. To get into the habit of regular daily meditative prayer or affirmations are an essential part of my mind to communicate with and receive guidance from the Infinite Intelligence in my subconscious mind. My research to get the most of this approach to the spiritual essence of God's Intelligence belief tells me that it's like training a dog with repetition. It is the same way the subconscious mind will accept and adopt God's will and logical purpose to put into action his plan for me. In no small way I "came to believe in a power greater than self " (AA Step 2) to give up alcohol and "handed it all over to a Higher power" (Step 3), and the obsession for the drink left me. It seems now the same methodology is required for rekindling the logical belief of the Trinity of Father, Son and Holy Spirit, as the Church advocates. So, like AA Step 11: "Sought through prayer and meditation to improve our conscious contact with God as we understood God, praying only for knowledge of God's will for us and the power to carry that out." Meditating on God's will every day, and having absolute faith and belief that what he has in mind for us will come to pass is already the key. I now believe using this technique will, over time, establish for me a direct connection to Infinite Intelligence via my subconscious mind. This takes the pressure of attempting to define God's creation to apply in my life. It matters little if the Infinite Intelligence, God if you will, started the whole show with a Big Bang. Was the force gasses in the void who lit the fuse or if by mutation in nature caused the origin of the species to eventually evolve to make Adam Ape.

We have him become aware that something other than thick wit was going on, and that he had a higher intelligence than the other barrel of monkeys. And appealing to the ego of this first man, Eve monkey gave him the forbidden fruit off the tree of knowledge and that is where I'll leave off. It seems to be that I cannot define God , find proof of his existence nor really pity into words the meaning of it all. Suffice to say that there is an Infinite intelligence that I choose to call God, in whom I trust as the creator and field force of my life's purpose. But now, what of my belief in the existence of Jesus Christ on earth, his guiding light of spiritual grace and place as " the Second Person of the Trinity" ? Thinking again of Pope Francis' Credo and his "'want to believe in God, and Jesus the Son," I realize that my manifested Christ only covers my creative mind belief but does little for the logic of his presence "I believe; help my unbelief"(Mark 9:24) How can this man say he believed in a manifested (risen) Christ and at the same time ask for help in overcoming unbelief? Well logically I need to provide some proof of his being here, to cement the faith in his supreme sacrificial act of dying on the cross for it is written that by his death and resurrection he redeemed the world.

It is a hypothesis, that the belief and non belief in the birth, death and resurrection and Ascension of Christ has comparative myth and fact. As far back as the ancient Maya recording and interpretations of the sky, was the belief that the will and actions of the Gods could be read in the Stars, Moon and Planets. The Maya believed that the Earth was the centre of all things, fixed and immovable. The stars, the Moon, Sun, and the planets were Gods. These planetary 'Gods' and their movements were seen as going between earth, the underworld, and other celestial destinations. These Gods were greatly involved in human affairs and their movement was watched closely. Certain traceless moments like a war or a mighty ruler's ascent to the throne would be delayed or advanced only when a certain planet was visible in the sky. In much the same way, the ancient Aboriginal culture told their stories from ancient Gods, animals and plant growth patterns. With perhaps one exception, the Aborigines retold these stories through to the 20th Century, of the birth of a certain God, who had a son from a black star in the skies , the son star died and left a spirit star for the tribes to follow. That star being the Evening star which is the brightest star forever more in the eastern skies of Australia.

Ultimately, the Maya ascertained that the Sun was the most powerful of all the planet Gods, and would shine in the sky all day before transforming into a Jaguar at night and passing through the Mayan underworld. It was the Maya who recorded the Sun dying (eclipse) in the sky and would remain in the underworld for three days before rising again in a new spiritual realism. Like man before and after the Mayan dynasties, who often claimed they descended from the Moon but worshiped the Sun, their most important planet was Venus, which was associated with battles and wars. Captured warriors and leaders would be sacrificed according to the position of Venus in the night sky. The Maya painstakingly recorded the movements of Venus and determined the year, relative to the Earth and not the Sun, was 584 days long, amazingly close to the 583.92 days that modern science has determined, when using a similar trajectory.

Moving from the misunderstandings of the 'Gods' of the ancients, and their myths of belief in a Sun God, the questions of copy-cat biblical stories of the Christ is nothing more than a plagiarist repeat of the stories of Horus, Krishna, Mithras, Dionysus and other pagan Gods, retold up to the time of the Roman 'God' Octavian. Octavian, later called Caesar Augustus, perpetrated a myth to keep a rabble distracted, alluding to the belief that he, 'Augustus' was the real Christ, the sacrifice lamb of the peoples of the Roman Empire and the Jewish 'heathen.' He, who would be adored as the one true God and everlasting in their lives and the hereafter.

It has been considered by modern day writings, possibly totally mythical, that Augustus, the then Roman leader Caesar Augustus, after the murder of his foster father Julius Caesar, had scribes record the myth of himself being 'Messiah.' He manufactured the story, having Saul, a Roman soldier, go forth and recruit followers after his so-called 'conversion' on the road to Damascus. If one was to believe such a 'story'- this may have occurred before Christ ascension into heaven. However, the Bible in Acts, clearly indicates Saul (St.Paul's) conversion occurred well after the Ascension. It is a moot point and really is essentially trivia: a case of the story of Christ on earth can not be proven or disproven, much less the case for Caesar Augustus being the true Messiah! There is more documented evidence, in the Bible and other credible recorded literature that confirms the reality of the Christ on earth story. Myth or reality, modern day man is either a believer or a disbeliever. I have my doubts about a living Christ on earth but stand to be corrected. A living Christ is an inward thing, I have come to accept this as a belief. Be it Christ in the manifest of Roman times, Christ in the biblical account that pacifies the brain of traditional believers or a Christ of one's own imagination is not the concern. The dead Christ can only, to my mind, be a Christ of the imagination, of an inner consciousness- a manifestation, whatever realm one chooses to follow.

It is not my task here to throw out the baby with the bathwater, but merely do my best to grow an embryonic manifestation of the Christ spirit for myself and give you, dear reader, words to consider on this subject. My writings before this occurred well after my return to Australia from my third Camino. As I have previously stated, my mind of The Way was a healing mind, an enquiring mind and the mind of a skeptic wanting to believe in something other than that the world I grew up in and indeed the current material world, other than a ' 'Santiago Traveling wanderer ' has to offer. So the text surrounding the signs of the Zodiac, the parallels relating to past spiritual leaders, doctrinaires of faith and morals, the signs in the planets, in the end count for little more than a puff of smoke in the reality of the now. I guess I begin to see what Christ reportedly said 'The kingdom of heaven is within.' When one deconstructs the Christ of miracle, mystery and authority, it is a short step to wondering if the whole story of Christ is a myth. Thinking on that premise, and the deepest construct of a creative human spirituality, the historical Jesus, as such never existed. However, very few in history and biblical studies draw the conclusion that a Jesus of the old story never existed. The main division in scholastic concerns is how to appropriate Jesus. Was he an apocalyptic or a wisdom-centred teacher? Few researchers question if he ever lived. Still, on a popular level, Jesus, understood as a myth, and strictly a myth, seems to be gaining ground. So, was he or wasn't he? Did he ever live or is it all just a good story? Critical examination of Christian gospels, especially with the rise of formal criticism, does recommend the conclusion that Jesus as the centre of Christian dogma emerged in the itinerant preaching of the earliest Jesus movement.

Basically, people spoke in the manner of the 'living' Jesus who had died. Preachers spoke 'in the spirit of Jesus,' thus making him alive in their witness. The Gospel of John is historical in the sense that it records the 'speaking in the spirit of Jesus.' This was the charisma of the early Church which, of course, eventually needed to be regulated in some form. The earliest social movements related to Jesus preserved his memory in this way. The parables and aphorisms of Jesus are a case in point. The forms of speech of this 'historic' Jesus, a base mode of teaching, was preserved, if re-interpreted, in the teaching and preaching of the next generation. Formal criticism was all about finding the voiceprint of the teacher that wascarried forward in new shapes, by students of this form. Now comes the myth. It all starts by asking how much of the Jesus material is fictional, arising from later generations who spoke 'In the name of Jesus' without actually saying anything the historical Jesus said. Also, how much of the Jesus material can be identified with confidence as an originating voice point, something close to historical? The line between these two questions is often blurry, and it is exactly this blurriness that inspires the possibility that all the material is mythical, that is, all the material is made up 'in the name of Jesus.' Once that step is taken, the natural conclusion is that there is no historical Jesus. It is actually hard to prove there was a historical Jesus using conventional forms of history. Jesus was unknown. We have to remember that the big name of his lifetime was Socrates. Everybody, including Jesus, had heard of Socrates. He was famous. Jesus, as a Galilean of his time was not famous and had no chance as his birthright of ever being famous. In the light of the rise of Christianity it is hard to imagine that Jesus was an unknown.

He may have been illiterate and poor as was his community. No one was able to hire scribes to read great works to them, to record great thoughts or send letters home. Still he was a carpenter's son so he would have perhaps understood mathematics and his reported knowledge of preaching to the scribes in the temple proves otherwise. The Christian gospels record the popularity of Jesus and his large following is almost certainly imaginary. His crucifixion by the Roman authorities was done without blinking-another nobody in a long line of nobody rabble rousers. We look at Jesus from the perspective of 2000 years of history, and he seems to us to be among the greats. Indeed, he is amongst the greats, but the immediate experience of his life belongs to a minor school or movement that was largely ignored and mostly unknown. Accordingly, it is not possible to expect a great recovery of contemporary witness to his life and times.

What we can expect is second- and third-generation historians mentioning him in light of a new and rising movement that claims him as the true Caesar (the Lord, Saviour, and the Son of God). Ancient historians and those not so ancient question : who was this Jesus and who were his people? Later historians know about the rising movement and relay whatever information they can gather regarding its founder. The information is humble. It concerns the followers who called him 'The Christ' ; His relationship to another teacher named John the Baptist, that He was crucified, that His followers are poor and ignorant. That there were lies and rumours spread about Him. This is what we can read in Josephus, Tacitus, Suetonius, the letter of Pliny the Younger and others - Mar-ben Saparion, Lucian and Samosata to name but a few of the many.

So why then does the idea "that Jesus never was" persist and gains "in" popular assent? The answer is plain fact that despite the aforementioned, there is no contemporary witness to the Jesus of history. The earliest we can get is Paul, an educated Roman soldier, who said that Jesus was once historical (2 Cor 5:16) who met and knew 'the brother of the Lord.' (Gal 1:19). Still, it remains simply true that there has never been an eyewitness report about any incident in the life of Christ. This simple fact is often the foundation for believing Jesus was only purely a myth. The second element that supports the belief Jesus was a myth emerges because this belief is partially correct. Much about Jesus is indeed a myth. Really, much about anybody including our own self is mythical. With Jesus, like with Confucius or other ancient teachers about whom nothing really exists, myth comes with the package.

The earliest Christian movement did interpret Jesus in the light of Jewish scripture; especially the prophets. The dying and rising of Jesus is consistent with the notion of divine intervention in pagan Gods, biblical reference-where the notion of regeneration is prevalent. Jesus, his death and resurrection, fits right in with these common, and universal, mythical patterns. Early educated Christians could draw upon both Jewish, Greek and later Roman sources in this regard. Thirdly, it is a plain fact that many early Christians preachers spoke in the name of Jesus, saying things that Jesus never said. Christianity created a cache of Jesus sayings that contained both historical and non-historical inspired sayings about the nature of Jesus, his divinity and the realm of the Kingdom of God. Whilst the commentary on the parables is made up, the use of parables is not. Jesus never said 'I and the Father are one.' (John 10:30) but rather he used a parable like 'a sower went out to sow his seed.'(Mark 4:3). and Mark did interpret the sower parable as an allegory about the quality of Christian believers. So, even within the Christian sources that witness Jesus, much of the witness is myth.

There is not much any historian can do about this situation except to understand it. Still, it does not prove the case that Jesus never existed. We all want something to believe, and sometimes when we used to feel certain about becoming questionable, the reaction is to throw the whole thing out. I guess I felt this way in the year my whole world seemed to come unhinged. I believed many things about my life from childhood to adulthood that turned out to be a myth. It all seemed to unravel in one year, some two decades ago. In that year there was a complete breakdown of my family tree. A long standing marriage was desecrated to the dust, and was tragedy to befall me and mine.

A wedge between young and old took an evil hold and I stood by and watched the fruits of my labor, my then perceived reason for living, wither on the vine. When I recovered from my sadness and madness, I discovered in my new adulthood things about myself and my family, my then value system that was all myth. I discovered that the mantra I lived by, the code of ethics I subscribed to, the 'story' I had told myself since childhood to get by and survive, to a great degree were not true. In fact I had been, to a large degree, living a myth, without recognising it as such. The human truth of the Jesus I was taught to believe in as a child varied greatly to the Jesus that now evolves within.

When the historical Jesus becomes someone who can inspire us and teach us about life outside Christian myth. This involves, and perhaps is the consequence of the act of forgiving Jesus for being human. It is part of his fate, to be one of the greatest myths of human history. But this does not erase the voiceprint of a historical figure. True, it makes Jesus an enigma, but it does not eliminate the basic fact of his humanity. So on the scales of belief, my own and by further investigation, like an anthropologist digging up some unidentified bones and trying to make some sense of the find, I endorse it. Not so much from a historical aspect but from agreement of factual verification of believers.

CHAPTER 3.

THE CHOICE IS ALWAYS OURS

I returned to journal down some beliefs that have evolved over the centuries in support of what Winston Churchill stated about Russia at the end of WW11- 'It is a riddle, wrapped in a mystery, inside an enigma.' Mine being more an endorsement to the existence of Christ breaking the riddle, unwrapping the mystery, which leans to fact more than fiction or enigma. God throughout the Bible spoke through the prophets to prove he was God. He foretold the future, taught them to verify who he was, to prove to people that those who spoke were true prophets, and to draw mankind to worship him only. The 100% accuracy of the prophecies that can be uncovered in the Bible that came true are proof of the existence of God and of Jesus if one opens the mind to these documented proofs.

'I am God, and there is none like me. Declaring the end from the beginning, and from ancient times the things that are not yet done saying, 'My counsel shall stand, and I will do all my pleasure:' (Isaiah 46: 10-11). There are many hundreds of perditions that have come true from the time of Christ, 30 AD until today. Perhaps the most pertinent right now are those that relate to Russia and the nations of Islam. Predicted ca. 10th Century BC: Psalm 120:5-7 predicted that Russians and Arabia would be a people that hate peace and embrace War. Fulfilled in 600 AD to the present for Arabia: when the Arabian prophet Muhammad spread his new religion of Islam, he used wars to do it and his followers have been warring ever since. Russia is still warring today but the ultimate war will come in the future as prophesied in Ezekiel 38-39, when they will lead a group of nations to fight Israel. It is to be hoped that the request of Our Lady of Fatima to pray for the conversation of Russia in this 21st Century will stave off this biblical prophecy. It is to be hoped that Vladimir Putin, if he retains power in Russia, will be a prayerful catalyst to help save the planet from a pending Nuclear war.

One must hope as a non believer that this comes to pass and as a believer that Putin is not living a KGB deception using the old Russian Orthodox Church as a cover for an even bigger future plot. Let us trust that he is the man of prayer that he seems to adjudicate by his current actions. The past biblical predictions do not leave one with much comfort for the future. Per haps the predictions of Christ that have come to pass will give some reassurance to this doubting Thomas and to other Pilgrims of the road of life towards eternity. Jesus reportedly, did not only fulfil prophecy in his own life time, he predicted coming events that were to come to pass in the future. One of the ministries of Jesus was that of the prophet. As has been true with prophecies fulfilled in his lifetime, his prophetic words have been literally and marvellously fulfilled!

Here I was back on the road again on another Camino. Trudging once more the well worn pathway to Santiago de Compostela. I was somewhere north west of the City of Leon, and stopped at Villar de Mazarife, at a small cafe on the side of the Way; some 21 km journey was more than enough for me for that day. It was mid afternoon and still quite hot. Finishing my cup of coffee I made my way to a nearby church to meditate. In the cool of a Chapel of God, reaching into my backpack, consulting my journal of notes I had taken that day for a quick review. Certainly I had written copious jottings on the historic Christ on earth and fulfilled predictions of the existence of God the Father: but had I justified the spiritual Christ reality? I knew I would review and expand on my writings with further research on my return to Australia from this Camino journey. But, on a scale of judgment of myself, had I reviewed enough of the Christ reality to balance the scales between belief and non belief; sitting in my lofty heights of self-righteousness reading between the lines? Indeed, what of the proof of Christ's existence, his predictions and his miracles? For that matter, what of the life and times of his disciple James the Stronger, who reportedly walked The Way I now trod? This was a story I didn't really believe but had made a note to further investigate, as I now planned to do on Jesus on my return home. I figured I still had a long way to go to rest my case, as I needed to rest my weary head, on my way to Santiago. Once more to journey to the end of the Way, out of darkness into light? To visit the Cathedral where I had first had my doubts about St. James ever visiting Spain let alone preach of his leader Jesus the Nazarene. At the Cathedral, despite my doubts, I had confessed my wrong doings, received absolution from a priest and eaten the Communion host. Yet. I had returned to that Cathedral on my second Camino in a worse spiritual state than my first, with no thought of forgiveness in my heart, no participation in the midday Mass ceremony.

The closest I got to a spiritual experience in that Cathedral and on the Way was to once more visit the crypt of St. James under the altar of the Santiago Cathedral, put my arms around a statue of his image above the altar and spend my time in Santiago investigating the purpose of the Mass, the Ark of the Covenant, and the host of Christ in communion. Investigating the 'smoke- belcher ' ceremony and the reverence that one might hold for the reenactment of Christ's last supper in the Mass and the golden Tabernacle on the Altar.

My current state was perhaps worse than my first and my second visit to the Cathedral, for I was lost in a time and a space warp, somehow in a void between the fantasy and the reality of a Christ-like existence. I resolved to do more research on this Christ figure, on St. James reported life and purpose on the Camino, to see if I could swing the scales of Judgement more to a justice of belief than unbelief, to perhaps renew the courage of my former faithful convictions or to drop the whole bundle as a useless exercise.

Could I uncover historical facts from secular sources as well as Christian, that Jesus was real and existed? Also that he is the most documented and historically verifiable figure in antiquity? I had done a fair job in my journal on God the Father, I thought, now how about his son? To get real verification, I turned once more to the library of words in sacred manuscripts and books I had purchased in bookshops and carried with me on this now more realistic inward journey of the Way. I first turned to Josephus, who did not believe Jesus was the son of God, but wrote about him. I decided to work my way through the many secular historians who lived in the century after the death of Jesus who confirmed his existence, Flavius Josephus being the first.

Titus Flavius Josephus (37-c. 100), a first Century Roman-Jewish historian and hagiography of priestly ancestry recorded Jewish history, with special emphasis on the 1st Century AD and the First Jewish-Roman War, which resulted in the Destruction of Jerusalem and its temple in 70. His most important works recount history of the world from a Jewish perspective for an ostensibly Roman audience. These works provide valuable insight into 1st Century Judaism and the background of Early Christianity. Josephus was a Jew who did not believe in Jesus Christ as the Son of God or Christianity.

In 'The Antiquities of the Jews', book 18, chapter 3, paragraph 3 this famous historian writes: "Now there was about this time Jesus, a wise man, if it is lawful to call him a man, for he was a doer of wonderful works- a teacher of such men as receive the truth with pleasure. He drew over to him both many of the Jews, and many of the Gentiles. He was (the) Christ; and when Pilate, at the suggestion of the principal men amongst us, had condemned him to a cross......"

Josephus goes on with further proof as to the condemnation of Christ. Josephus, considered one of the greatest historians of antiquity, independently provided proof and evidence of Christ's reality confirming the biblical account as well.

Cornelius Tactus was a Roman Historian who lived from 55-120 AD wrote the following passage that refers to Jesus, called 'Christus', which means 'The Messiah', in book 15, chapter 44 of The Annals. After a six day fire burned much of Rome: 'Consequently, to get rid of the report, Nero fastened the guilt and inflicted the most exquisite tortures on a class hated as an abomination, called Christians by the populace. Christus, from whom the name had its origin, suffered the most extreme of penalties during the reign of Tiberius at the hands of procurator, Pontius Pilatus. Titus goes on to describe how the followers of Christ like him perished. Despite the fact that he clearly despised Christianity as a 'mischievous superstition.' Tacitus no less confirms once again the existence of Jesus and his crucifixion on the cross, it also states Pontius Pilate as the procurator who oversaw the crucifixion again giving non- Biblical proof of Jesus' existence as it is recorded in the Bible.

Plinius the Younger wrote of the Persecution of Christians. Gaius Plinius Cascilius Secundus, (61AD –112 AD) better known as 'Pliny, The Younger' was a lawyer, author and magistrate of Ancient Rome. He wrote numerous letters to such notables as Tacitus and the Emperor Trajan. He was considered an honest and moderate man, consistent in pursuit of suspected Christian members according to Roman law, and rose through a series of Imperial civil and military offices, the cursus honorum- imperial sequential order of office. In correspondence with the Emperor Trajan he reported on his actions against the followers of Christ. He asks the Emperor for instructions dealing with Christians and explained he forced Christians to curse Christ under painful torture. So not only was Pliny aware of Jesus Christ, he also provided a description of the activities of the early Church. In later writings he details persecution against Christians.

Sextus Julius Africanus (c.160-c.240) was a Christian traveler and historian of the late 2rd and early 3rd Century AD. He is important chiefly because of his influence on Eusebius, on all the late writers of Church history among the Fathers, and on the Greek school of chroniclers. Julius Africanus quotes about writings of Thallus, who was the first non – Christian historian. In his Chronicles, Africanus quoting the historian Thallus, explains the reason for it being so dark during the time of the day of the crucifixion of Jesus Christ: as 'an eclipse of the sun.' Non-

Christian proof of Jesus' existence and another confirmation of the Bible's account of Jesus crucifixion.``

The Bible states a reference to the time Jesus was put on the cross which is confirmed here: 'now from the sixth hour there was darkness over all the land until the ninth hour.' The sixth hour is noon and the ninth hour 3 pm.. Thus we see that the historian Thallus was trying to explain the odd occurrence of the sky being dark at noon when the crucifixion of Jesus took place as an eclipse. Africanus also quoted Phlegon, a Greek historian who lived in 2nd century AD and also wrote of the eclipse occurring on the day Jesus was crucified. This again confirms non Christian sources that confirms the account of Jesus being a real person who lived as well as confirming the account of his crucifixion straight from the bible. And another Bible quote: 'at the death of Christ, the sun darkened , the earth trembled and the dead arose and appeared to many.'

Lucian (Born 115AD) was a well known Greek satirist and a traveling lecturer. More than eighty works bear his name. He mocked Christians in his writing, but at the same time provided evidence that Jesus was real. 'He was second only to that one whom they worship today, the man in Palestine who was crucified because he brought this new form of initiation into the world.' He goes on to describe the belief of Christians, the personal sacrifices they make, their transgression from denying Greek Gods to worship this Christian God. And being all on one level with this God in their belief for eternity.

Lucian does not mention Christ by name but he confirms his existence that he was crucified in 'Palestine', had followers who believed in eternal life and that they were equal in Jesus Christ. Lucian even mentions that Christians deny all other gods and believe in 'faith alone.' This again is in accordance with the Bible's clear statements about the Christian faith and provides more evidence of the existence of Christ, that 'the man in Palestine, did really exist.'

Gaius Suetonius Tranquillus, known as Suetonius (ca.69/75)- was a Roman historian belonging to the equestrian order era in the early Imperial era. His most important surviving work is a set of biographies of twelve successive Roman rulers from Julius Caesar to Domitian, entitled 'De Vita Caesarum'. In the apparent description of his writing he states- "The Emperor Claudius reigned 41AD to 524 AD.' Suetonius reports his dealings with the eastern Roman Empire, that is, with Greece and Macedonia, and with Lycian, Rhodesians, and Trojans. He then reports that the Emperor expelled Jews from Rome, since they constantly made disturbances at the instigation of Christ." Skeptics will point to the different spelling to say that's not the Jesus he's talking about. But again, with the totality of evidence, it's obvious that followers of Jesus in the Roman Empire were persecuted by Roman authorities. It certainly falls in line with other chronicles and biblical historical parchments that the Romans who followed Jesus were being punished for it.

There is a great logical fallacy among Bible skeptics, atheists and those who challenge Christianity that says, when discussing historical aspects of the Bible 'you can't use the Bible as proof that Jesus existed. You use non- Bible sources!' To which this author says ' Well, why not?' The four Gospels of the Bible are bibliographical accounts of the life of Jesus. The normal objective measure of the reliability of historical documents is 1. the number of available copies of ancient manuscript. 2. the time span between original versions and the date of those copies that are still in existence today. When examined under this standard, the Bible proves to provide a treasure trove of proof and evidence that Jesus really existed. All other non-biblical historical evidence supports and reinforces this. Manuscript fragments of the New Testament documents, written between 50-100 AD, support all the biblical and non-biblical evidence of the existence of Jesus Christ.

The record of life, ministry, death and resurrection of Jesus Christ has more evidence and proof than any other person from antiquity. Jesus believed that he was just a regular man but he was reportedly the son of God, who gave his life on the cross that so many historians knew about, to take the punishment for the wrongdoings of humanity. It takes faith and trust in that sacrifice to receive him. Jesus said: 'Behold, I stand at the door and knock: if any man hears my voice, and open the door, I will come in to him, and will sup with him, and he with me. To him that overcomes will I grant to sit with me in my throne, even as I also overcame and I sit down with my Father in his throne.'- 11 Revelation 3: 20-21. Jesus obviously wants us to believe in him based on volumes of documented evidence of his birth, death, resurrection, and ascension into heaven. If we are to be free from our defects of character, we have to be committed in our lives here and now to have eternal life in the hereafter and reign with him. So having now established that He existed, what is it that he is really asking of us? I began to ponder this thought. Still determined to further delve into the matter of faith now and not the evidence of his existence.

Did I really need to do that though? What is it that this God of my inner spirit is asking of me? I was thinking. Jesus in the scriptures particularly the Sermon on the Mount, in Matthew's gospel points out the essence of his teaching: Jesus is consistently seen to be merciful, gracious, faithful, forgiving, and steadfast in love. Of course, it is not always easy on a daily basis to live by this Credo.

But if Jesus is the image of his Father i.e. the Universal God figure that is nonetheless hard to believe in his existence in the void, and we are called to imitate him-then it stands to reason that the way to live by these principles is to bring those five adjectives into play. So practicing mindfulness as Christ dictated in his Sermon on the Mount is to appreciate the need for his grace- that gift that can only be absorbed by doing unto others as they would have us do unto you. Those five adjectives of mercy, grace, faith, forgiveness and steadfastness seem to be the catalyst of human action for the betterment of oneself and our fellow man. If that's all there is to it, then it's worth a shot to try this Christ credo for a better life- being a believer or a non believer.

Jesus was only on earth as a man for a short time. He was visited by shepherds as a witness to his coming for they had been told already by an angel of his birth. Likewise Magi Kings had followed a star from the east to the place of his birth, offering gifts of gold, frankincense and myrrh. Apart from his preaching to the priests of the temple at age 12, he goes missing for 18 years and next appears when he returns from 40 days of fasting in the desert and is baptized by John the Baptist in the River Jordan. He preaches for the next three years to his followers performs many miracles, predicted future events, and ultimately sacrificed himself on the cross for the wrongdoings of mankind, died and was buried at age 33, rose again from the dead three days later, visited his followers and ascended into the heavens. Jesus not only fulfilled his own spoken prophecy in his lifetime, he predicted events that were to come to pass some time in the future. One of the ministries was that of a prophet. Jesus had predicted that 'heaven and earth will pass away, but my words will not pass away' (Mathew 24:35)- these words still echo throughout Christendom, read and believed by untold millions. Mary of Bethany poured oil on the body of Jesus in her anticipation of his death. She was rebuked by the disciples for wasting the oil. Jesus chastised them saying that her story would be retold wherever the gospel was preached. This has always come to pass.

Jesus also predicted that one of his own would betray him. This was literally fulfilled by Judas. Jesus predicted that Peter would deny him three times before the cock crowed. This too came to pass. He predicted that he would suffer at the hands of religious rulers. On the night he was arrested the religious rulers allowed him to be beaten. Jesus predicted he would die in Jerusalem and upon a cross. Both predictions took place. He predicted that he would die during the Passover and would rise again in three days. This is well documented as having occurred as he predicted.

Many other events such as the destruction of the City of Jerusalem within one generation, the destruction of the Temple, the scattering of the Jewish people from their land, their captivity and the ruling of the Holy land by the Gentiles, the persecution of the Jewish people and though persecuted, the nation of Jews would survive all of these predictions have been literally fulfilled. These facts demonstrate beyond any doubt that Jesus was indeed a genuine prophet. During his earthly ministry Jesus touched and transformed countless lives. Like other events in the life of Jesus, all his miracles were documented by eyewitnesses. The Gospels record 37 of these and are mentioned in various texts by the four writers Mathew, Mark, Luke and John. The ability at age 12 to interpret holy scriptures and teach wise scribes and priests in the Temple of Jerusalem would seem like a miracle to them at the time. He went on to perform many miracles over the remaining 3 years of his remaining time on earth before he was crucified. This was followed by healing the sick, casting out evil spirits from the possessed, cleansing those diseased; restoring the use of limbs, restoring the sight of the blind and hearing of the deaf; calming the sea, ensuring a major fish catch, feeding the multitude, walking on water, bringing people back to life and many more.

So it was that I came to believe and relive the logic of the symbolism of the Church teachings of my youth without actually embracing the Church, and learnt to hand over and trust in a manifested Christ of my own understanding in the creative imagination. To this day, this trust has worked as an untold miracle for me in handing over to that power. "I" of me so to speak, and the healing power of AA has helped me stay sober a day at a time to the present day. Others may have a Buddhist view as their Higher Power, some may have the Almighty God of Mohammad's message to cling too, still others may have a view of the reality of nature as their guiding power, whilst some may simply depend on the healing power of AA in any meeting or some may well struggle sitting on the fence so to speak and are as yet to embrace a Higher power. It is not for me to judge, but it is my job to trust in what I embrace as a higher power, within the Steps of AA and in particular Steps 3: letting go and handing over to the God of my understanding and Step 11; Meditation and prayer in my conscious contact with God, and Step 12 having had a spiritual awakening, try to carry the AA message to other still suffering alcoholics. .

I was back in real time now as I entered the courtyard once more of the Cathedral of Santiago and was struck by the amount of restoration work that was going on at the front entry to the building towers. I later noted that the two side entrances and the rear of the Cathedral were covered in scaffolding with a curtain of blue to reduce the dust from the cleaning of the ancient stonework. This was in stark contrast to the past two times I had finished my Camino's. The Church was spending millions on this historic structure whilst beggars lined the doorways with cups in hand pleading for a handout. Nothing is static I thought, not even the modern changes to an ancient icon could take away from the celebration that takes place at the pilgrims mid-day Mass, not even the coin I slipped into the beggars cup, not even in the multitude of Pilgrims who have for over a thousand years tramped their way here.

Looking at the great pillar that stands at the main door of the Cathedral, I had hoped that I would see the worn stone of hand prints of the thousands of Pilgrims that had entered the Cathedral and had placed their hand there. So many hands had gripped the pillar inside the Cathedral front door since the Medieval times that they have worn a hand like groove into it. Disappointed, I realized by the surrounding scaffolding still encasing the pillar that it was still under restoration as it had been, on my first visit to the Cathedral in the summer of 2013. I made my way to the entry under the altar to the reported remains of St. James and joined the line of Pilgrims there to worship a myth. The reported Saint's remains, encased in a silver casket beneath the main altar, visited by so many Pilgrims lined up for hours far beyond the entry doors to the Cathedral. Above and behind the altar is a narrow staircase where Pilgrims climb to the decorated bronze statue of St. James to embrace his shoulders and kiss his mantle. There were far too many Pilgrims lined up like lambs to the slaughter, so I decided to wait for a quiet hour to check it out again, despite my belief that all that the Pilgrims were celebrating is a myth. The myth of the mans' bones lying below the altar, the legend of James as the 'Moor Slayer' and the folklore surrounding the wisdom of him preaching his mantra "faith without works is dead' has reached a crescendo once again in this 21st century as it did in Medieval times. One might expect a blessing for the visit there, but I was just a tourist visiting a mythical relic. This visitation to the shrine in the Cathedral is not the only attraction for pilgrims of all faith and but those of no faith at all. In fact the biggest attraction in the Pilgrims Mass itself is to see the famous 'botafumeiro' in action, the "smoke-belcher," the largest censer for spreading incense in the world. Weighing 80 kg and 1.6 meters in height, the huge censer is swung on a pulley system above the altar with ropes requiring eight men to get it to reach speeds of up to 80 kilometers per hour. It is said that the censer was installed to cover the stench of the many unwashed pilgrims that congregated for the Mass in medieval times. It does have a more religious cognition as incense has been employed in worship by Christians since antiquity.

All my indoctrinated Catholic teaching from my childhood was returning as I stood there in that Cathedral. Yes, we do need myth, legends and folklore to give us a spiritual sense of a power greater than ourselves that runs this show. I reasoned that the symbolism of St.James remains, the Catholic rituals during the holy sacrifice of the Mass and the consecration of the host as the 'Body of Christ' and the wine as the 'Blood of Christ' was the greatest symbol of all for a spiritual reconversion for any true believer. But here I was still a doubting Thomas, as to the true meaning of Jesus and a Higher Power escaped me. As did the mission of St. James and the reported relics that lay in the crypt under the altar.

That I doubted James ever walked the Spanish landscape in a mission of conversions of those early cult believing Galatians of the Iberian coastline was of little consequence. Those Spanish fisherman, farmers and traders back then were more interested in ancient witchcraft than some stranger who preached of the crucifixion of a man who claimed he was the Son of God and died for our sins. It was the middle of the Mass for Pilgrims and the incense was burnt as a sacrifice in prayer rising up to God. I recalled that it is commonly used in the celebration of the Eucharist, at Solemn Vespers, Solemn Evensong, at funerals, benediction and exposition of the Eucharist. Chinese Taoism, Buddhism and many other religious faiths use the burning of incense for similar purposes, in medical healing and meditation ceremonies. I somehow suspect that the large "smoke- belcher" used in the Cathedral is more to attract the pilgrim crowds to the Mass celebration than its religious or historic use. Whilst St. James crypt, his statue and the censer bring the Pilgrims to their final Christian destination at Compostela de Santiago, it is by no means the real reason for the celebration of the Pilgrim Mass. The Tabernacle at the altar and the host that is housed within, when not being served at communion, has a deeper historic and religious significance than any other part of the Mass service. This is somewhat overlooked in the euphoric celebrations for the pilgrims at the Cathedral at the end of their pilgrimage.

The Tabernacle or "dwelling place," according to the Hebrew Bible, was the portable earthly dwelling place of God amongst the children of God from the time of the Egyptian Exodus through to the conquering of Canaan. The inner chamber, within the Arc of the Covenant, housed two tablets which inscribed the Ten Commandments, as revealed by God to Moses in the desert. Moses broke the first tablet in anger upon returning to camp, where he discovered a Golden calf which followers were idolising. The broken and intact tablets are reportedly within the Arc as well as Moses' walking pole which had produced a living branch after Moses' dialogue with God at the burning bush. My mind returned for a moment as the Priest turned from the altar and blessed the masses of pilgrims, who like me maybe, stood in quiet desperation. I thought of Henry David Thoreau's quote : "The masses of men lead lives of quiet desperation."

I thought of my recent life's experiences and remembered another Thoreau quote. One that was a favourite long before I took the road less traveled and ended upon the Camino Way. " If a man does not keep pace with his companions, perhaps it is because he hears a different drummer. Then, let him step to the drummer that he hears; however near or far away."

The Priest turned to the Tabernacle on the Altar of the Santiago Cathedral at the Pilgrim's Mass. The new Judaism, founded on the death of a Sacrificial lamb, Jesus of Nazareth: a carpenter's son who died that we may live. A modern day Ark of the Covenant I mused; as I watched the Priest drink the remainder of the wine in the chalice and crumbs of the host after serving the privileged pilgrims who had eaten of the flesh and drank of the Blood of Christ. The Priest placed the remaining host into the Chalice and the altar boy poured more wine he swirled the Chalice around as an experienced wine connoisseur would do, and drank. The Priest further cleaned the silver vessel with gold lining, with a sacred cloth, placing the Chalice with leftover hosts in the Tabernacle. Then he drew the curtain veil across the gold Tabernacle door, closed and locked it. Kneeling, the

Priest prayed silently for a moment. Then he turned to the multitude of pilgrims now ready to walk out of their darkness of the Way, traveling into a new beginning, renewed light, traveling with the Christ of their own understanding, he stated "Go in peace, the Mass is ended...thanks be to God."

How important to me is or was that symbol of the Ark of the Covenant, I was thinking as I walked from the Cathedral? Did I belong to the Old Testament ways or the symbolism I was indoctrinated to believe in? Or was it my lot now to traverse a greater path of discovery taught by myth, legends and folklore in the Old Testament and the New? "Just hand it all over Doug." I heard an inner voice say. I was somewhat relieved but for a moment, and despite my doubts, felt that I should have denied Catholic tradition and taken Communion anyway. My mind had drifted back to another time. The Passover feast was one of the main Jewish holidays and a celebration in remembrance of God's deliverance of the Israelites from bondage in Egypt. In fact the slaying of the Passover lamb and the applying of the lambs blood to doorposts of houses is a beautiful picture of Christ's atoning work on the Cross.

At his last supper it is written Jesus said, as he broke bread and gave it to his Apostles " Take this bread and eat it for this is my body" then he took a cup of wine and said "Take this cup and drink it for this is my blood." " Unless you eat the flesh of the son of man and drink his blood you shall not have life in you. He who eats my flesh and drinks my blood has life everlasting and I will raise him up on the last day." A heavy burden for this pilgrim's inner truth.

The last words are from Peter 1:18-21 " For you know that it was not with perishable things as silver and gold that you were redeemed from the empty way of life handed down to you from your fore-fathers but with the precious blood of Christ, a lamb without blemish or defect. He was chosen before the creation of the world, but was revealed in the last times for your sake. Through him you believe in God, who raised him from the dead and glorified him, and so in faith and hope are in God." The significance of the Tabernacle in the Cathedral at Santiago and the host of the Body and Blood of Christ served as a communion of the faithful during the Mass celebration far out weighed the celebration of the "Smoke-belcher" and the visitation to the bones below the crypt which I had visited now on three occasions in my Camino.

CHAPTER 4.

SYMBOLS AND SIGNS

Making my way back to the Cathedral late in the day I knelt before the reported bones of a disciple of Christ, who supposedly knew the man and set out to preach his word in foreign lands, as the story goes. Whilst I did not and still do not believe the bones are St. James, I still knelt and said a prayer just in case my version of the James relic myth is fact. Once more I was caught up in the spectacle of the Mass, listening to the peaceful hymns and looking at the masses of mankind attending the celebration.
I could not but still help thinking of myth, legend and folklore that surround the Church, the Jewish faith and even the Bible itself. I obviously have a long way to go on this journey inward and the outward symbolism of a Church steeped in tradition seems quaint but antiquated in this age. This was my third visit to the Cathedral but somehow I just could not get into the swing of it all. On my first visit, the Church had been packed when I entered
and a voice had called then. It was Nicole, an English beauty I had met along the Way. She said " I knew you would come and I've saved a space for you."
Nicole was always talking about strange things happening on her Camino. She had walked the Way once before with her sister. I had expressed some unusual events that occurred in and around me on my Camino. Nicole always answered with "That's the Camino." I recalled, as I sat next to her, the celebration of the Mass was far from my thoughts back then. I began to recall my next visit and remembered taking up most of the Mass time checking out every pew to see if Madeleine was there. She had disappeared like a ghost from my site on the Way and I wondered if my mind was playing tricks on me. At that Mass celebration I was certainly not focused on the one true faith I was indoctrinated into as a child. Maybe my thoughts were more influenced by the cult of Christianity than the Sacrificial Lamb at that time. My soul seemed to be with a spiritual Christ within, a Higher Power of which I am still learning to trust. I pray that my influence was more God centred than cult.
It is both the Church symbolism and the Risen Christ, the God of the Manifest, that keep me of sober mind and of spiritual duties in logical acceptance and imaginary observance of faith in a power greater than self. A Tabernacle

on the altar from my Christian upbringing is a representation of the Jewish Temple and the slaughter of the lamb performed by a layman, followed by the rituals dealing with the blood and fat which had to be carried out by a priest in the Jewish historical tradition. The priest in turn cooked the flesh of the lamb on the altar and the smoke essence that rose from the cooking to the heavens above was an observance of the assembly in worship. They were given the flesh of the lamb to eat as a symbol of their faith. In much the same way Christ reportedly offered himself as a living sacrifice for the sin of man, and the body and blood of Christ is kept in the form of a bread and wine and eaten by the faithful in commemoration of Christ's living sacrifice.

The Tabernacle of the Catholic faith, if you will, symbolize the Jewish temple altar of the old testament and Christianity is the new Judaism. So to the Stations of the Cross around the walls of the church tell the story of Christ's ordeal for mankind, as do the statues of the Virgin Mary and the saints. Even the church and its architecture has that symbolism. As I was educated to this, or rather indoctrinated to it in my youth, it is natural for me to gain some peace in such a place without necessarily following the religion of my youth. It is like the logic of the symbols and signs of my former faith having a head justification of a belief in the Higher Power, but my creative brain sees the God particle as a manifested Christ who is risen, and in whom I can hand over too. But how did I arrive at this having turned agnostic for many years in my adult life, and for a little while reached a scientific come atheistic cynical view of non belief. Well, it was when I could no longer take the itch that I could not scratch to align me with the Third Step of AA that I knew I needed a Higher Power to embrace. But what of the logical linear view, the scaffolding of belief that I was educated too, once embraced as a basis for my belief from childhood to adult life.

It seemed timely as I revisited the Santiago de Compostela Cathedral to reconsider the meaning of all through its symbols, relics and architecture. It was no different to other historic Catholic Church that I had visited in the past, but I needed to refresh my memory of its significance to me. The church has always been symbolic of the body of Christ. How can one explain the body of Christ by measuring it in meters, cataloging the material and the building techniques used in constructing an edifice? The major part of the studies which today are dedicated to Christian temples treat the symbols quite briefly, if at all. They limit themselves to classifying information concerning materials used, aesthetics and the function of the building. If one is to believe in the Catholic faith doctrine, then the Church was born with Christ, its doors have been open to the world for about two thousand years and will remain open until the Parousia, the Second Coming, when they will close forever and the Last Judgment will begin. For everyone: for those who will be within and those who will be left outside. After the Last Judgment, there will no longer be any reason for the temple to exist, as has been written in the Apocalypse of John of Patmos, because in the sacred City, in the heavenly Jerusalem, the Temple will be God Himself.

I entered the gathering space, frequently called the narthex, the place where the faithful greet one another before and after Mass. It is the area between the outside doors of the church and the inner doors leading into the worship space. This is where we are welcomed each Sunday, where baptisms, funerals and weddings begin; here we form lines for processions and receive palms. In the early history of the Church the narthex was a waiting area for non baptizsed individuals and penitents not allowed inside the worship space and not allowed to participate in all or part of the Mass, for religious literature and for parish notices or displays. Throughout the centuries the restrictions on Mass attendance have been relaxed, but the term "narthex" remains. In the gathering space we, at least mentally, discard our secular ways, knowing that we are about to enter holy ground and that our attitude, body language and even our attire reflect the sacredness therein.

The nave is not a meeting place but a place of worship; the congregation is not an audience but participants in the Holy Sacrifice of the Mass. In most churches today, the nave is filled with pews or chairs. That was not always the case. For over 1,000 years, churches did not have seats for the congregation; the faithful mostly stood or knelt during the Mass. Not only did they stand, but they were separated by gender. Men were normally on the right facing the altar and women were on the left. Not until the 13th century did pews or benches become popular; still today there are Catholic churches without seats, save a few designated for the old and the ill and even our attire reflects the sacredness therein. The word "nave" comes from the Latin "*navis*," meaning ship. According to Catholic teaching We, the people of God, are regarded as passengers on a ship destined for heaven. Parishes quickly discovered that pews are an expensive addition and the cost of installation was passed on to parishioners. Pews were purchased or rented by the laity and often regarded as the property of a particular person or family.

This idea persisted for centuries. Today we may contribute to pew renovation or installation, but we don't own a particular pew (although many of us seek to sit in the same spot at every Mass). Next is the Sanctuary. "They shall make a sanctuary for me, that I may dwell in their midst" (Ex 25:8). The sanctuary is the area, often raised, in the front of the church where the altar, the ambo, the celebrant's chair and, in many churches, the tabernacle are located. Separated from the nave, this is the place reminiscent of the Holy of the Holies, that is, the inner sanctuary of the temple described in the Old Testament. Interestingly, the altar and tabernacle were centuries apart in their introduction into the Church. The General Instruction of the Roman Missal defines the sanctuary as "the place where the altar stands, where the word of God is proclaimed, and where the priest, the deacon and other ministers exercise their offices" * *The sanctuary's elevation above the nave floor serves to enhance the view of the laity but also exemplifies a special, sacred place. The Al*tar is the centrepiece, the most important part of the church to which everything else is subservient. Every Catholic church is built for the altar. Altars have been part of religious services going back to antiquity, even before churches were built; the name altar is derived from a Hebrew word meaning "place of sacrifice." Well into the fourth century, there were no churches nor public worship. Christians held their divine services away from the occupying Romans in places like private homes. Often the altar was a simple wooden table or chest.The top of the altar, called the *mensa*, a Latin word for table, traditionally has been made of stone. The altar is consecrated by a bishop and becomes the symbol of Christ: "The stone that the builders rejected has become the cornerstone" (Mt 21:42).

The Catechism of the Catholic Church defines the altar: "On the altar, which is the centre of the church, the sacrifice of the cross is made present under sacramental signs. The altar is also the table of the Lord, to which the People of God are invited" (Canon Law No. 1182). Here for us is Mount Calvary; here too, the bread and wine are turned into the body and blood of Christ. * *In the early Church, altars were built on the sites of martyrs' graves. As more churches were built, relics were contained in or buried under altars, a practice that still occurs today.* Since there were no churches during those early centuries, Christians did not have a tabernacle. However, as we do today, they were careful to protect the Blessed Sacrament. There is some evidence that following their divine services, Christians took the consecrated bread home and consumed it during the week. By the fourth century, when construction of churches began, any reserved hosts were kept in various rooms in the church, including an area that became known as the sacristy. Theft, pilferage or worse was a serious threat, especially following the Protestant Reformation, when violence was carried out against the Church.

The design of the tabernacle slowly evolved, and by the 16th century tabernacles similar to those we have today were in use. Canon Law spells out the rules for the tabernacle's location: "The tabernacle in which the Blessed Eucharist is reserved should be sited in a distinguished place in the church or oratory, a place which is conspicuous, suitably adorned and conducive to prayer" (No. 938.2). As authorized by Church law, and approved by the local bishop, some churches use a separate chapel to house the tabernacle. The tendency today is to keep the tabernacle in proximity to the altar.* *Wherever located, the tabernacle is always locked and immoveable in order to protect the Eucharist. * Wikipedia*

In every Catholic church we find a readily visible lamp or candle burning before the tabernacle. This is the same light the Magi followed until they found the baby Jesus in a stable. This ever-present light still beckons to each of us. We all look for the flickering flame as soon as we enter the church. Our attitude and demeanour change as we recognize that we are in the house of the living God. The flame signifies his presence and a sign that our love for the Lord is eternal, never to be extinguished. Called the sanctuary lamp, it was first used in the 13th Century, and Canon Law 940 requires the lamp to burn continuously. This perpetual light is mentioned in Leviticus 6:6 in discussing the fire for burnt offerings: "Fire shall be kept burning upon the altar continuously; it shall not go out." * *The flame of the tabernacle lamp is purposely transferred from candle to candle beginning with the fire lit at the Easter Vigil Mass.* Wiikpedia.*

During the Mass, the ambo is the focal point for the Liturgy of the Word. From this kind of tall, elevated desk, "only the readings, the responsorial psalm and Easter proclamation (*Exsultet*) are to be proclaimed; it may be used also for giving the homily and for announcing the intentions of the prayer of the faithful" (General Instruction of the Roman Missal, No. 309). The design and location of the altar and ambo emphasize the close relationship between the Liturgy of the Word and the Liturgy of the Eucharist: from the holy altar we receive the body and blood of Christ, and from the ambo, Christ's holy doctrine. In this regard the ambo, like the altar, is not just an object but a sacred place. The General Instruction of the Roman Missal also explains: "The dignity of the word of God requires that the church have a place that is suitable for the proclamation of the word and toward which the attention of the whole congregation of the faithful naturally

turns during the Liturgy of the Word." Once the persecution of Christians ended in the fourth century, churches were built and designed with an ambo or raised platform, making it easier for the congregation to hear. Around the ninth century, the pulpit replaced the ambo and was located either in the sanctuary or the nave.
* *Typically, early Church ambos had steps going up each side with an area at the top big enough for the reader and servers with candles to stand.* Wikipedia.*

During the Mass, the priest represents Our Lord Jesus, persona Christi, and thus the priest's chair is always distinguishable from other seats in the church. The chair is not designed as the place for a king; it is not a royal throne, not palatial, but it is easily differentiated from other chairs in the sanctuary and recognized as the place for the one who leads the congregation. The chair is always placed so as to be seen from the nave. "The chair of the priest celebrant must signify his office of presiding over the gathering and directing the prayer" (GIRM, No. 310).

* *In a cathedral, the chair is known as the cathedra, where the bishop exercises both his teaching authority and role as a successor of the apostles.* Wikipedia.*

Statues and pictures of Jesus, the Blessed Mother and the saints adorn nearly every church. Catholics don't pray to or worship statues; rather we venerate, we admire, respect and seek to imitate the individual emulated in the statue. We worship our living Lord, Jesus Christ, not his statue. The saints depicted in Catholic churches lived lives of heroic virtue and are now believed to be in heaven, where they can intercede for us before God.The statues, pictures, even the stained-glass windows tell about Jesus and the Scriptures. These images have long been an important educational tool, especially in the first 1,500 years of Christianity when few people were literate. Relics are treated in a similar way, as best explained by St. Jerome (340-420): "We do not worship, we do not adore, for fear that we should bow down to the creature rather than to the Creator, but we venerate the relics of the martyr in order to adore him whose martyrs they are."* *The Second Council of Nicea and the Council of Trent reiterated that the faithful venerate the person represented by the image and not the image itself.* Wikipedia.*

Baptism is the door to all the Church's sacraments. The baptistry or baptismal font is part of every Catholic Church and located so that the congregation can participate in the baptismal ceremony.Some fonts are large pools with free-flowing water and normally found as you enter the nave; others are smaller and placed in different locations. The early converts to Christianity were baptized in rivers, streams, public baths, some even in the catacombs. For the most part, it wasn't until the fourth century with the construction of churches that baptisms were brought indoors. Over the centuries, even until recently, the receptacle used for baptisms has been continuously reduced in size. The U.S. Conference of Catholic Bishops' document "Built on Living Stones" says for each parish that, "One font that will accommodate the baptism of both infants and adults symbolizes the one faith and one baptism that Christians share." * *The Church today approves the use of either triple immersion for baptism or the pouring of water three times over the candidate's head. * Wikipedia.*

The Easter (or Paschal) candle is located near the baptismal font, the exception being during the Easter season when it is placed next to the ambo. Originating around the fourth century, this large candle represents the light of Christ, and a new Paschal candle is blessed during each Easter Vigil. It is lit for every baptism, and the flame, the light of Christ, is transferred to a candle given to the baptized individual or to an adult family member when an infant is baptized.

* *The Easter candle is also lit during a funeral, recognizing that the deceased shared in the death and resurrection of Jesus at their baptism. *Wikipedia.*

From the Latin word *sacristy*, meaning a room near the sanctuary or church entrance, this room contains the bread and wine, sacred vessels, the books, the vestments, everything needed in the celebration of the Mass. It is the location where the priests and ministers vest. The sacristy was part of the church since the first places of public worship were built in the fourth century. Here the sacred vessels are cleaned after Mass.* *In most sacristies there is a sacrarium, a sink that drains directly into the earth where water from cleaning the vessels is poured. This is to ensure that the safeguard of any residue of the sacred body and blood of Christ's host is not mixed with unholy drainage residue. Wikipedia.*

In nearly every Catholic Church, 14 Stations of the Cross ring the walls of the nave. We can walk along with Jesus as he makes the agonizing journey from Pilate's house to his crucifixion on Calvary that first Good Friday. We halt at each station meditating on the actual or traditional events that took place at that particular spot. This most popular devotion evolved over several centuries.

While many Catholics participate in this devotion every Friday of Lent, the stations are available for us to "walk" any time. " We adore thee O' Christ and we pray, for by thy crucifixion you have redeemed the world." (My speech in recall). * *The Stations of the Cross varied in number until Pope Clement XII (r. 1730-40) settled on 14 and identified the events associated with each station.*

Each church stores holy oils for use in various ceremonies. New oils are blessed annually during Holy Week by the bishop at the chrism Mass and then distributed to parishes. The oils are: the oil of the catechumens, the oil of the sick and the chrism. They are kept locked in an aumbry, a French word meaning wall safe or cupboard. Our Catechism says, "The sacred chrism (myron), used in anointing as the sacramental sign of the seal of the gift of the Holy Spirit, is traditionally reserved and venerated in a secure place in the sanctuary. The oil of catechumens and the oil of the sick may also be placed there" (CCC, No. 1183).* *Today the aumbry takes different forms and shapes and often is located near the baptismal font. * Wikipedia*

The first Christians confessed their sins face to face to a bishop in his church and in some instances to the congregation. Public confessions were short-lived and stopped by Pope Leo I (r. 440-461), who wrote: "It is sufficient that the guilt which people have on their consciences be made known to the priests alone in secret confession." Face-to-face confession, typically kneeling before a priest or sitting in a chair at his side, was the norm until the middle ages when a screen was placed between the confessor and female penitents. This action eventually led to the introduction of the confessional booth in the 16th century, which included the screen separation, and from that time until the Second Vatican Council, confessions were normally anonymous. In 1974, the Church introduced a new formula for confession, which promoted a reconciliation room instead of a confessional booth. Penitents could now go to confession face to face or behind a screen.

  I was on my own road less traveled on this Camino to Santiago. Thousands of travellers had walked this pilgrimage before me, and no doubt many would do so in the future. This was a time for reflection and introspection; unexplained happenings; logic giving way to myth and legend. In the clear daylight of this plodding journey, towards the end of my Camino Way, I found myself recalling the events of my Camino journey and the events of a past life that was now but a dream; a film implanted in my memory, that no longer held emotions – just simple recall. Visions of which, had I reentered, would have resulted in feelings of joy, pain, sadness, love, hate – or, in fact, any of the deadly sins that are biblically spoken of. I resolved to not go there now, but rather to focus on the steps of my travel on this hot Spanish morning. My thoughts somehow drifted to my inner "Sword of Discernment" and who I really was and what I am now all about; the mindful image that I had logically determined and sought to have some outward symbol of, had seemed to be a worthy quest to fulfil on my journey. It was to be the outward fulfilment of a myth at the end of the rainbow at Santiago which, through accomplishing my inner mission, would result in me completing and producing a result that would be worthy of my cause. It was proving to be another myth, buried upon yet another myth. The inner movement of my thoughts, emotions, feelings and desires were, in fact, more of a mindfulness of sharp spiritual perception and judgment. My becoming sensitive to my ever-changing movements and understandings were questions that came from I knew not where, nor, in fact, to discern where they were leading me to in a spiritual sense.

I had returned to the Cathedral de Compostela on my last day in Santiago to attend the midday Mass. Arriving before the celebration began, I walked through the nave area where pilgrims like me were already gathered in quiet prayer and anticipation of the coming event. Wandering around the outer rim of the nave I stopped to take in the many confessional boxes side by side along the walls. Above each was a sign written in a foreign language, inviting pilgrims to have their confession heard by a priest of their nationality or tongue. I stood for a long time gazing in wonder at the sign that said in

English, partly in awe of the meaning of confession and the fact that it had been a long time since I had my slate of soul cleaned in the presence of a priest and received absolution, in the Name of the Father, Son and Holy Spirit. I was taken aback at the antiquated ways of this Santiago parish Cathedral, for it was still living in a past of Canon Law pre Vatican Council 11 (1962-64). When at home in Australia one could go to a priest in an open confessional sitting in a room face to face, as opposed to the former way. Still, believers had their right to go to confession the old way if they so desired or embrace the new. Deep in thought at the anomaly of present opportunity of confession the new way and not the past hidden behind a screen, I was awakened to the voice of a priest who approach me and spoke in English: "Hullo, would you like to go to confession?" He followed that up quickly by saying : "Follow me." Thinking perhaps it was a sign from Jesus in following in his footsteps, I followed. The priest was of Spanish extraction spoke fluent English and told me a little of his life and struggles in following the ways of his creator. We were seated opposite each other in a large sanctuary room of the main nave area, as he coaxed me into confession. I used the historic : "I confession to Almighty God" approach and guessed at how many years it had been since my last confession.

Using the typical AA template when sharing, I proceeded to tell him what it was like in my past life, sharing my defects of character, what had changed in my struggle to be God centred, and what it was like now. He listened thoughtfully, granted me absolution from my sins in the name of the Father, Son and Holy Spirit, and ushered me into a private chapel to prayers in penance for my former wrongdoings. Whilst I had only recently walked the 800 km of Camino letting go of past burdens, rising from the darkness into a new life so to speak, that confession had lightened my spirit.

On my way home to Australia I decided to spend a few days in Madrid to take in the historic sites, and visit a museum of Spanish art. On my wandering around the city I ventured into another Cathedral to check out the architecture and take some photos. The Cathedrals in Spain, as in all Catholic Churches, including our own in Australia, are a reminder to me of the inter connection between the iconic designs within and the features that to me were more in the making of man as a template in design of meaning, of Jesus the Son of God and his sacrifice for all. The shape of the inner sanctum is in likeness to that of a man as to the crucified Christ. Entering the 'narthex,' gathering space of a waiting for the non baptized. Unworthy individuals not yet ready for entry to the main body of the holy of holies. To me it represented the lower nature of my physical self of carnal desires. Thus, in retribution and forgiveness I could now venture into the body of the Church in likeness to Christ body, this holy ground of the gathering of his people, the body of Christ. I looked to the left area of the altar like it was an arm of the lord, being the gospel side. Then to the right lay a large Bible on the lectern was in readiness for epistle lessons. To the centre being the altar and the tabernacle housing the Holy Eucharist. It was a sign for me that God's son Jesus was the head and the church of its people was the body of Christ. I thought of my physical passions and my spiritual needs and heard the words in my head "God is the head and we are the body, and it is the head that rules the body and not the body who rules the head."

I thought of the historic significance of the tabernacle and its representation to the grace one receives in the partaking of the Eucharist in the reenactment of the last supper, Christ's sacrificial act in dying for our wrongdoings, as I had a sudden urgent desire to partake of the communion host. The Mass had been well un derway as I continued to take photographs. The priest turned to those present in the congregation, took the host from the chalice, held it high above his head and called: "Behold the Lamb of God, behold him who takes away the sins of the world. Blessed are those called to the supper of the Lamb." And the congregation replies:. "Lord, I am not worthy that you should enter under my roof, but only say the word and my soul shall be healed. I found myself making my way to receive communion for the first time in decades with a repeated mantra all the way to receive the host: " Look not upon my sins but the faith of your Church." I heard the priest say"Body of Christ," as he administered the host and as I partook of the body and blood of Christ I said " Amen," meaning " So may it be."

It was a further afterthought that Christ had died that we may be dubbed his present day messengers as 'The body of Christ in his own image and likeness.' I then imagined that with a One world of communion body of people we could be the catalyst to his 'Second Coming,' for the ultimate salvation of the people of faith. For he may well come as a unification of our spiritual body inasmuch as a physical presence. I approach a group of young pilgrims I recognised by their scallop shell Camino patch on their back packs standing in a group after Mass outside the Cathedral. I was in need of sharing my elated spiritual experience having just received communion, feeling in a state of grace. I introduced myself, explained the fact that I had just arrived from another Camino and mentioned that I had shared in their Mass sacrificial act by receiving communion for the first time in years. I was in so much need of sharing heightened enlightenment. They were an excited young group who wanted to know all about my Camino and invited me to join them for lunch at a nearby restaurant. We spent some hours together and their company was a highlight of my day. I left them with the ever familiar farewell expression on the Camino Way "Buen Camino," meaning 'good journey.'

The Mass of that day soon faded into oblivion, for on my return to Australia. I got caught up in life's distractions once more. The heightened spiritual experience of the Mass and communion in Spain soon faded into the light of creativity but not the doctrine of faith and morals. Although I continued to practice the suggested steps of Alcoholic Anonymous and the ways of my justifiable manifestation of a God of my own understanding.

So it took time to get to where I am at now with the balance of logic and linear mind being embraced with the creative spirit too. And now that I have returned to view the Church's teaching in a different light by examining its Credo of belief, I find myself entering the logical and linear meditative aspect of its mystery as much as my creative mindset of handing over to a power greater than self. And so the Catechism, Credo and Canon laws I continue to examine.

I write now in God speak, or more to the point in Bible text as it is believed and relate to the people who follow the Catholic faith. As in the Book of Genesis 9 God willed to make men holy and save them, not as individuals without any bond or link between them, but rather to make them into a people who might acknowledge him and serve him in holiness. He then therefore initially chose the Israelites race as his own people and established his covenant with them : Then God said to Noah and to his sons with him: "I now establish my covenant with you and with your descendants after you and with every living creature that was with you—the birds, the livestock and all the wild animals, all those that came out of the ark with you—every living creature on earth." Book of Genesis Chapter 9. It is further confirmed inActs 10:25: "But in every nation whoever fears Him and works righteousness is accepted by Him." So he gradually instructed this people as a prelude to the new and preparation to the new and perfect covenant which was to be ratified in Christ…The New Covenant in his blood; he called together a race made up of Jews and Gentiles, which would be one, not to the will of the flesh, but in the Spirit. In the same way, after supper he took the cup, saying, "This cup is the new covenant in my blood; do this, whenever you drink it, in remembrance of me." Cor 11:25.

I am reminded of a hymn that is often sang in the Mass celebration, about the oneness of God's people. I think it sums up the essence of what a Universal is all about.

One bread, One body,
One Lord of all,
one cup of blessing
which he blessed,
And we though many
throughout the earth,
we are one body in this one Lord.

Gentile or Jew, servant or free,
women or man m no more.
One bread, One body,
One Lord of all,
one cup of blessing,
 which he blessed.

CHAPTER 5.

GOD'S PEOPLE & PROPHETIC BELIEF

So in Catholic doctrine the people of God are marked by characteristics that clearly distinguish them from all other religious, ethnic, political, or cultural groups found in history. Moreover it is believed that God is not the property of any one people, but he acquired a people for himself from those who were not a people: " A chosen race, a royal priesthood, a holy nation." (Peter 2:9). It's thought that one becomes a member of these people not by physical birthday, but by being "Born again," a birth of "water and the Spirit," by faith in Christ and Baptism. So it follows that the people have for its Head Jesus, the anointed one, the Messiah. Because, the same anointing of the Holy Spirit flows from head into the body, this being the people of Jesus. Those who practice the faith enjoy the dignity and freedom of being sons of God, in whose hearts the Holy Spirit dwells as in a temple. So the spiritual mission of embracing the Holy Spirit is to be"the salt of the earth and the light of the world." Matthew 5:13-16. A people in destiny, finally, [is the Kingdom of God, begun by God himself on earth, which by his countenance to be further extended through the actions of his people until it has been brought to perfection by him at the end of time.] In summary, Jesus is the one whom God anointed, and through his sacrificial act grants his people the Spirit and grace, as priest, prophet and king. Thus, the whole people of God participates in these three offices of Christ and bears the responsibility for mission and services that flow from them. In being embraced as the People of God through faith and baptism, we share in the uniqueness of priestly vocation; Christ as high priest had made his people a kingdom of priestly duty to God, the Father. The baptized, by regeneration and the anointing of the Holy Spirit, are consecrated to be a spiritual house and holy priesthood.
(Hebrews 5:1-5.)
The People of God share also in Christ's "prophetic office," above in the supernatural sense of faith that belongs to the whole People, lay and clergy, when it "unfailingly adheres to this….once for all delivered to the saints." (Jude 3.) And when it deepens its understanding and becomes Christ's witness in the midst of this world. In embracing the priestly duties,the mission of Christ prophetic office,

we the people of God come to share the 'royal office of Christ the king. He exercises his kingship by drawing men to himself through his death and Resurrection. Christ is King and as 'Lord of the Universe,' made himself a servant of all, for he came " not to be served but to server, and to give his life as a ransom for many." Matthew 20:28. For Christians," to reign is to serve him," particularly when serving: the poor and the suffering, in whom the Church recognizes the image of her poor and suffering founder." The people of God fulfils its royal dignity by a life in keeping with its vocation to serve with Christ Jesus.

I was reminded of the epilogue I delivered at my son Peter's funeral some two decades ago. He was just 26 when he died by his own hand, and it was in keeping with doctrines of faith that I said: " I am the vine and you are the branches, and some of us are branches, some of us are leaves, and some of us are falling leaves, and some of us are fallen leaves; and we all come under the power of the Sun, and the Father, the Son and the Spirit are one. I guess I was at the time indicating that we are all one inspirit and in nature. No one is beyond being saved in the eyes of God if we embrace the sacrifice of Jesus and accept that we can be received by the grace of the Holy Spirit. It was a wayward attempt to reconcile my belief in an hour of great pain and suffering.

In truth I was once more doubting Thomas finding little relief from grief except in the continual habit of regular drinking alcoholically. I was back in time in my mindset when I had grave doubts about the Catholic faith's teachings and standing on my lofty agnostic height whilst still attending Mass, viewing those who attended Communion as non thinking sheep or more critically lambs to the bidding of the churches indoctrination. The years that have since passed have softened my attitude, as I have come to believe in the Almighty Power of God and the spiritual gift of receiving the host of Jesus Christ. The gift of the sacrificial lamb in the reenactment of the last supper, and the Crucifixion in Holy Communion. [And he claimed a mysterious and real communion between his own body and ours: " He who eats my flesh and drinks my blood abides in me, and I in him."] John 6:56. Further consider his visible presence was taken from his disciples, he did not leave them orphans. He promised to remain with them until the end of time. .{'He promised to remain with them, who eat of the flesh and drink of the blood, to the end of time, and sent the Holy Spirit.' (John 14:18,20-22; Matthew 28:20; Acts 2:33). The Holy Spirit being the essence of his sacrifice of his body and blood in the crucifixion to forgive us our wrong doings, as we consume the host, doing this in remembrance of him. So this communion with Jesus has become more intense "By communicating his Spirit, Christ mystically constitutes as his body those brothers of his who are called together from every nation. (Luke 7.)

The comparison of the Church with the body cast light on the intimate bond between Christ and his Church. Not only is the Church gathered around him as a unit, but is united in body. The three aspects of the Church as the Body of Christ are to be more specifically noted : The unity of all its members with each other as a result of union with Christ; His being the head of the body, and the Church as the bride of Christ. So it is that believers respond to God's word and become members of Christ Body, become intimately united with him: " In that body of the life of Christ is communicated to those who believe, and who, through the sacraments, are united in a hidden and real way to Christ Passion and " really sharing in the body of the Lord,...we glorification. Luke 7 again. Thus firstly in Baptism, which unites us to Christ's death and resurrection, and the Eucharist, by which 'we share in the body of the Lord,...we are taken up into communion with him and with one another." (Romans 6:4-5, Corinthians 12:13.)

The Catholic scripture uses the phrase "the Body of Christ " to indicate identity, oneness and unity in Christ. When people believe in Jesus' death for the sins of the world and in His resurrection, they are joined to Christ in his death and resurrection (Colossians 2:12). So in the building up Christ's Body there is a diversity of member believers and functions. Firstly, the one Spirit gives according to his own grace the needs of his ministries, the gifts for the welfare of the Church. The unity of the Mystical Body of Christ produces and stimulates charity among the faithful: " From this it follows that if one member suffers anything, we all suffer. And if one member is honoured we are all honoured, then all the members can rejoice. (Corinthians 12:26.) For it is written in the unity of the Mystical Body that he triumphs over all human divisions. " For as many of you who were baptized into Christ have put on there is neither Jew nor Greek, there is neither slave nor free, there is neither male nor female, for we are all one in Christ Jesus." (Galacians 3:27-28).

It is for me hard to accept and fathom how the Church in its doctrine can promote its views of faith and morals, being restrictive to the benefit of receiving the Eucharist members for those in the "state of grace" who practice its strict Canon law to practicing Catholics only and not those of other faiths. Further, it is fair to say that renegades like me, who do not fit the bill of the Church orders in matters of faith and morals in receiving the Eucharist have their own interpretation. Under Church 'rules' we are condemned and not supposed to go to receive the Eucharist because by living contra to traditional beliefs having been divorced, are still intimate in a relationship outside of marriage, or have not confessed their sins to a priest in order to obtain forgiveness, we cannot receive the Eucharist in our participation in the holy

Sacrifice of the Mass. Firstly, it is my opinion that any good Christian should be more than welcome to participate in a Catholic Mass and receive The Eucharist in accord with their own belief. The Church is supposed to be for all and whilst it boasts of being a 'Universal ' Church, it does not, to my mind, practice what it preaches in Ecumenism concept and principle that Christians who belong to different Christian denominations should work together to develop closer relationships among their churches and promote Christian unity. And that includes receiving the body and blood of Christ duringMass. Just saying. For it is a matter of conscience of the individual who, to my mind, can pray for forgiveness directly to God prior to receiving communion and bypass the priest in that regard. Admittedly, one does not receive absolution from the priest after confessing, Traditionally the priest absolved the penitent sinner using the formula "I absolve you from your sins in the name of the Father and of the Son and of the Holy Spirit." But in the Mass itself, the priest turns to the people holding the Eucharist, offer an invitation: "Behold the Lamb of God, behold him who takes away the sins of the world. Blessed are those called to the supper of the Lamb." The assembly response is : "Lord, I am not worthy that you should enter under my roof, but only say the word and my soul shall be healed." The 'sinner' says in mantra-like fashion: "Look not upon my sins but the faith of your people." We are one with God, our intention is honourable in the receipt of the Holy Eucharist, so leave that judgment to God and not to man. (Doug speak).
Christ sent his Apostles so that the ' repentance and forgiveness of sins should be preached in his name for all nations." Luke 4:47. He further stated to his Apostles: " Go therefore and make disciples of all nations, baptizing them in the name of the Father and the Son and the Holy Spirit." (Matthew 28:19). So it was as reported in the New Testament that Jesus chose the Apostle Peter to be the foundation stone of his Church: " Thou art Peter and upon this rock, I will build my church, and the gates of hell shall not prevail against it." (Matthew 16:18).

So it was that the centre of Christianity since the foundation of Saint Peter's Basilica by Constantine (4th century), has become the later stage of the permanent seat of the Popes, the Vatican. It is the pre-eminently holy city for Catholics, an important archaeological site of the Roman world and one of the major cultural references. Fast forward to the first Vatican Council session which was held in St Peter's Basilica on 8 December 1869 in the presence and under the presidency of the Pope. The purpose of the council was, besides the condemnation of contemporary errors, to define the Catholic doctrine concerning the church of Christ. The sessions then continued at Nicaea in present-day Turkey, the council established the equality of the Father, the Son, and the Holy Spirit in the Holy Trinity and asserted that only the Son became incarnate as Jesus Christ. The Council of Nicaea was the first council in the history of the Christian church that was intended to address the entire body of believers. It was convened by the emperor Constantine to resolve the controversy of Arianism, a doctrine that held that Christ was not divine but was a created being. The Arian leaders were subsequently banished from their churches for heresy. It was there that the Nicean Creed was born. The First Vatican Council issued only two decrees, the first, Dei Filius, on the relationship between faith and reason, and the second, Pastor Aeternus, on papal primacy and infallibility.

Then in 1962 Pope John XXIII called a meeting of another Vatican Council stating that the purpose of the Council was the "modernization of the Church after 20 centuries of life." This refreshening of the Church's traditions is commonly referred to as aggiornamento ("bringing up to date" in Italian). The council was convened to respond to the rising influence of rationalism, anarchism, communism, socialism, liberalism, materialism, and pantheism. It's purpose was, besides this, to define the Catholic doctrine concerning the Church of Christ. As a result of Vatican II, the Catholic Church opened its windows onto the modern world, updated the liturgy, gave a larger role to lay people, introduced the concept of religious freedom and started a dialogue with other religions. Among the Pope's stated objectives in calling the council were: to foster spiritual renewal; to renew commitment to world evangelism and develop strategy; to lay the groundwork for an eventual reunion of the Catholic Church and other Christian denominations; to make church doctrine more accessible and comprehensible. Among the many changes, the Mass once said in Latin for many centuries, until the Second Vatican Council called for the prayers and instructions of the Catholic Mass to be translated into the local vernacular.

In the 10 years after the Council 100,000 men left the priesthood worldwide. Once the walls of custom and reverence that had surrounded them were broken, there seemed nothing to keep them in. Both Vatican 1 and Vatican 11 produced many documents that were in fact re-stated documents drawn from ancient doctrines of the church, which is the depository of the faith. Vatican 2 was longer and produced more documents ostensibly because Christian population had increased greatly by the time it took place (1963-65). However to many Catholics it had not moved far enough, the influence of the old school of those sticklers to the Canon Law of former days still held the upper hand within the Vatican chambers at the time and thus the Church held fast to the old at the expense of a spiritualistic evangelism that was sweeping the world at large. The only changes I saw as beneficial to the Mass attendees at the time, was that the Priest and the Altar faced the people, making the sacred sharing of the Eucharist more inclusive, and the Mass was said in English. I also breathed a sigh of relief that the Church's Easter dues list was no longer read from the pulpit by the priest on Easter Sunday any more. Formerly the priest would read from a large register how much each family contributed to the Church coffers: "Mr & Mrs McPhillips, two Guineas, Mr & Mrs Brown, One Pound, two shillings and sixpence, " and on and on the reading of contributions to the Church would continue. It was embarrassing for many who could not afford much, to hear their paltry contribution read out in public.

Apart from the old ways, there was the tradition of the seven sacraments that have not changed throughout the age of the Church. They are the Sacraments of Initiation (Baptism, Confirmation, the Eucharist), the Sacraments of Healing (Penance and the Anointing of the Sick), and the Sacraments at the Service of Communion (Marriage and Holy Orders). Each is celebrated with a visible ritual, which reflects the invisible, spiritual essence of the sacrament. Whereas some sacraments are received only once, others require active and ongoing participation to foster the "living faith" of the celebrant. Baptism is seen as the sacrament of admission to the faith, bringing sanctifying grace to the person being baptized. In Catholicism the baptism of infants is the most common form, but non-baptised children or adults who wish to join the faith must also receive the sacrament. A person is to be baptized only once in their life, and the Catholic Church recognizes baptisms done by most other Christian denominations as valid. In the rite of baptism holy water has been blessed by a member of the clergy and usually sprinkled or poured on the head of the child or adult when ministering the sacrament, simultaneously invoking the Trinity with the words, "I baptize you in the name of the Father, and of the Son, and of the Holy Spirit." The old self is said to die in the waters, and a new self emerges, mirroring the death and resurrection of Christ. Given that the sacrament is understood as a requirement for salvation, anyone, even someone who is not a baptized persons, can baptize someone as the situation requires.

The Eucharist, or Holy Communion, is another sacrament of initiation and can be received daily if desired. It is the central rite of Catholic worship. A baptized child's First Communion is usually celebrated around age seven or eight and is preceded by their first confession (the sacrament of Reconciliation). During the Mass the priest consecrates bread and wine, the elements of the Eucharist, which are 'converted' into the body and blood of Christ. As a memorial of Christ's sacrifice on the cross and in a reflection of his Last Supper with his disciples, the congregation then shares in the sacred meal. Special lay ministers (i.e., non-priests) are trained to bring the consecrated elements to the ill or otherwise homebound so that all Catholics can participate.

Confirmation is the third sacrament of initiation and serves to "confirm" a baptized person in their faith. The rite of confirmation can occur as early as age 7 for children who were baptized as infants but is commonly received around age 13; it is performed immediately after baptism for adult converts. A bishop or priest normally performs the rite, which includes the laying on of hands in prayer and blessing and the anointing of the forehead with chrism (holy oil) with the words, "Be sealed with the gifts of the Holy Spirit." In so "sealing" that person as a member of the church, the outward rite of confirmation signifies the inner presence of the Holy spirit, who is believed to provide the strength to live out a life of faith. At confirmation a Catholic may symbolically take the name of a saint to be his or her patron. Also known as Confession or Penance, the sacrament of Reconciliation is seen as an opportunity for renewal and can be done as often as needed. Some Catholics participate weekly before receiving the Eucharist, whereas others may seek the sacrament only during the penitential seasons of Lent, in preparation for Easter reenactment of the last supper, death and resurrection of Christ and his ascension into the heavens or at Advent, which is the preparation of the coming birth of Christ. Reconciliation is a means of obtaining pardon from God for sins (mistakes, or one might call defects of character) for which the sinner is truly remorseful, and brings the sinner back into communion with God and the Church. The sacrament is an opportunity for self-reflection and requires that the person take full responsibility for his or her sins, both those in thought and in action. During the rite, sins are recounted privately to a priest, who is seen as a healer aiding the process, and the priest commonly assigns acts of penance, such as specific prayers or acts of restitution, to complete in the following days. A prayer of contrition is offered at the end of the confession, and the newly absolved Catholic is urged to refrain from repeating those sins.

Anointing of the Sick, formerly known as Extreme Unction, is a sacrament that is administered to give strength and comfort to the ill and to mystically unite their suffering with that of Christ during his Passion and death. This sacrament can be given to those who are afflicted with serious illness or injury, those who are awaiting surgery, the weakened elderly, or to ill children who are old enough to understand its significance. A person can receive the sacrament as many times as needed throughout their life, and a person with a chronic illness might be anointed again if the disease worsens. The rite can be performed in a home or hospital by a priest, who prays over the person and anoints their head and hands with chrism (holy oil). The priest may also administer the sacrament of the Eucharist if the person has been unable to receive it and can hear a confession if so desired. If a person is at the point of death, the priest also administers a special Apostolic blessing in what is known as the Last Rites.

In Catholicism marriage is a sacrament that a baptized man and a baptized woman administer to each other through their marriage vows and lifelong partnership. Given that to a Catholic sacramental marriage reflects the union of Christ with the church as his mystical body, marriage is understood to be an indissoluble union. The rite commonly takes place during a Mass with a priest serving as the minister of the mass and as a witness to the mutual consent of the couple. The marriage union is used to sanctify both the husband and wife by drawing them into a deeper understanding of God's love and is intended to be fruitful, with any children to be raised within the teachings of the church.

Holy Orders is a sacrament that is available only to men who are being ordained as deacons, priests or bishops. As with Baptism and Confirmation, the sacrament is said to convey a special indelible "character" on the soul, the spiritual or non material part of a human being regarded as immortal of the recipient. During the rite, which typically occurs during a special Sunday mass, a prayer and blessing is offered as a bishop lays his hands on the head of the man being ordained. In the case of the ordination of priests and bishops, this act confers the sacramental power to ordain (for bishops), baptize, confirm, witness marriages, absolve sins, and consecrate the Eucharist. Deacons can baptize, witness marriages, preach, and assist during the Mass, but they cannot consecrate the Eucharist or hear confessions. With the exception of married deacons, an order restored by the second Vatican Council all ordained men are to be celibate.

So in summary. The purpose of the sacraments is to sanctify men, to build up the Body of Christ and, finally, to give worship to God. Because they are signs they are also instructions. They not only presuppose faith, but by words and objects they nourish, strengthen, and express it. That is why they are called sacraments of faith. The Church's faith precedes the faith of the believer who is invited to adhere to it. When the Church celebrates the sacraments, she confesses the faith received from the Apostles whence, the ancient staying: 'lex orandi, lex credendi applies,' i.e. The law of prayer is the law the Church believes as she prays. Liturgy is a constitutive element of the holy and living Tradition. For this reason no sacramental rite may be modified or manipulated at the will of the minister or the community. Even the supreme authority in the church may not change the liturgy arbitrarily, but only in the obedience of faith and with religious respect for the mystery of the liturgy. Likewise the sacraments express and develop the communion of faith in the Church, the lex orandi, the relationship between worship and belief, is one of the essential criteria of the dialogue that seeks to restore the unity of Christians.

From the moment a sacrament is celebrated in accordance with the intention of the Church, the power of Christ and the Spirit acts in and through it, independently of the personal holiness of the minister. Nevertheless, the fruits of the sacraments also depend on the disposition of the one who receives them. The Church affirms that for believers the sacraments of the new Covenant are necessary for salvation. "Sacramental grace" is the grace of the Holy Spirit, given by Christ and proper to each sacrament. The spirit heals and transforms those who receive him by conforming them to the Son of God. The fruit of the sacramental life is that the Spirit of adoption makes the fruitful partakers in the divine nature by uniting them in a living union with the Son, the Savior. Thomas Aquinas (1225-1274) produced a comprehensive synthesis of Christian philosophy that was adopted as the official in 1917. He summed up sacramental signs:"Therefore a sacrament is a sign that commemorates what is accomplished in us through Christ's Passion- grace; and "prefigures what that Passion pledges to us- future glory. " [St. Thomas Aquinas, Sth 111,60,3.]

74

There was a man
walked the streets of Leon
on the Camino Way.

He lived on love
for his follow man
claimed that he was free.

Words of love
sung in truth
an ancient philosophy.

There he told a story
how Jesus died in sacrifice
just to set us free.

And so he sang;

" There is no sin, there is no sin
there is no sin cried he
Just defects of character
And we must make amends."

We must learn to surrender
give into The Way
feel the sorrow in your heart
then let it slip away.

It does not matter
whose right or wrong
do what you must do
hand over to the Lord

There is no sin,
there is no sin
just defects of character
and we must make amends.

Doug McPhillips- Camino Way- 2017

CHAPTER 6.

WHAT DO THE RENEGADES DO?

As far back as I can recall I was indoctrinated to the sacraments of the Catholic Church. My introduction was to the doctrines of faith via my Baptism not long after I left the hospital crib. My mother more than my father wanted the initiation to be done post haste. Whilst Dad was apparently present when the priest poured the waters over my head announcing: " I name you Douglas John, in the name of the Father, the Son and the Holy Spirit." It was not the original name intended as both parents had their heart set on John Douglas by all accounts, but as there were a lot of John's being born at the time they switched the order. Perhaps as my life has proven, I would have been better to have retained the name John, meaning ' graced by God,' as opposed to Douglas, which means 'dark waters ' or 'thoughtful darker.' Much of my life has seemed to be destined to dark thinking. That is until I reversed the thought patterns to swing life as a glass half full and not half empty.

At age seven, having been entrenched to be physically disciplined into the instruction of the Catholic Catechism by the Sisters of (No) Mercy, and learnt Latin of the Mass by the rule of the Stock-whip, I received my first Holy Communion. This event was precipitated by my first confession to heal my soul before partaking of the host. By Catholic tradition, I had been cleansed of the original sin of my first parents, Adam and Eve; pronounced 'sin free' again by the parish priest prior in my first confession of healing to partaking of the host in communion, the body and blood of Christ. Like my fellow classmates at the time, we felt pretty special on our first Communion day. Especially when we celebrated the Mass and having Christ Jesus inside of us in communion, we were given a special meal followed by cake and cordial. Life was simple then and little boys did what they were told with the mantra "little children should be seen but not heard." We lived the rule of daily prayer, regular morning Mass attendance and conditioned to a world of charity for the less fortunate among us, many of who were Aboriginals who lived in government housing settlements north and south of our little community.

In the last year of my primary schooling we were instructed in the final step of initiation into the faith by becoming soldiers of Christ in a confirmation ceremony. It was a big deal of a day. The Bishop of Lismore, some three hours north by road or rail, came to officiate the event. We children of God, boys and girls, each lined up and knelt in turn before the Bishop who sat on a throne like chair in front of the altar half way through the Mass and questioned each in turn on our selected name for confirmation initiation as a soldier. I chose Joseph, being the foster father of Jesus, and found his presence in my mind's eye comforting in time of trial at the time. Years later, when my eldest son Scott announced 'Luke' as his choice to the Bishop, he was questioned about the Saint by the Bishop who assumed he had chosen 'Saint Luke." Scott was quick to point out to the Bishop that it was Luke Skywalker of Star Wars and not the Saint of the Gospels who was to be his guiding light. I sometimes think, considering his adult life, that Scott still has the Jedi Knight as his guide. God bless him.

So as I was marched off to boarding school at age 13 and the Marist Brothers who for the next 5 years of my teens ensured that the 500 boys at the time under their 24/7 care were regimented into the faith by the 'rule of the cane,' daily Mass attendance, confession and communion. I sometimes wonder how we fitted our religious practice in, considering sports training from 5.30.. Mass at 7 am, breakfast at 8, school work until 12 noon, a half hour lunch break and brief relaxation then back to class from 1 pm to 3.pm. followed by sport activities until dinner at 5.30 p.m.and study from 7 pm until 8 pm. Senior boys returning after 8.30 pm study until 9.30 pm. Lights were always out by 9.30 pm in our dormitories. In between we had to find time to wash our sports gear, socks, make our beds, clean our shoes and a host of other duties centred around our religious rituals. Our cleanliness habits included a brief shower in the morning and it was first in best dressed to get some hot water. The afternoon shower, particularly after football training, was a cold shower at the field sheds even in the winter months. Life was spartan like to say the least, as we proved to toughen up to the rigours of our way of life in preparation for the evils of the cold world beyond the walls of our school after graduation.

The practice of my religion was second nature to me from the very beginning of my career in the first year of life after death so to speak. I did my utmost to give an account of my stewardship by practicing the principles of the faith. However, my new career posted me beyond the bounds of church and parental influence and pretty soon I was just another wayward young man of the 60s thinking outside the bounds of belief and living the life of Riley. At least on the surface it seemed to be for I had discovered alcohol. Thus began my drinking which was more than acceptable in social outings by new found friends and work colleagues alike. Although I consistently drank to excess it was tolerated as so many of my fellow club bar companions dash did.. I still managed to go to Mass, confession and Communion on a regular basis and check out my wayward life with the local priest from time to time for spiritual guidance. Those of Irish descent were not too bothered with my drunken behaviour, as likewise they, more often than not had too much blood in their own alcoholic systems. The rot came fast in that first year as apart from the grog I discovered a wayward woman who enticed me to the 'power of the pussy,' and pretty soon the power of God went out the window, as did my regular religious practice. Mostly I attended Church outside of Mass hours deep in contrition before the altar asking for guidance, but only lessons of life with potential damnation got me back on the straight and narrow for a time.

My career life of the logical linear reasoning brain continued to rocket as I immersed myself into the doctrines of the protestant work ethic. That was tampered somewhat by my habits outside of work surrounded by those of like mind and of the drinking kind and girl friends who tended to come and go. I did get close to the altar in my late twenties, but interference from the mother of my bride to be who considered I was far too much like her Uncle Billy, a gambler, drinker and heavy smoker, that she interfered with marriage proceedings. So, licking my wounds, I took timeout from my career and headed overseas to sow the last of my wild oats before returning to Australia. I had a game plan for a management post with a large insurance company. I scored the job then made my way up the corporate ladder, found a young lady several years younger and after a one year courtship we married. She had not been Catholic, but to the delight of a Catholic priest she became one of us and we joined as two in one flesh in the sacred duties of a married couple.

My career role in life changed as I moved from corporate stooge to being an entrepreneur in my own business pursuits. This proved highly lucrative, affording our family the best of material success, private education for my children and the luxury of living in the fast lane of wealth and prosperity. For the first twenty years or so of the marriage we were relatively happy but my alcoholic drinking habits and workaholism in the pursuit of monetary reward, for no particular purpose other than being on a treadmill, got in the way of love and respect for each other over time. The last nine years of our marriage we were both desperately unhappy and ultimately the marriage broke down. We had tried to patch things up, putting on a front for friends and family, seeking marriage counselling and non professional advice but in the end it failed. I did my best to get her to return but she had already moved on and divorce followed with the dividing up of material spoils. That wasn't the end of it, a series of tragic circumstances followed over the next year, not the least of which was the death of my son Peter by his own hand. I tried to drink my way out of the suffering that brought but no amount of booze eased the pain.

For the next three years I turned to other women instead of to God. Ultimately another failed relationship and my now full blown alcoholism landed me in rehabilitation. It took a number of years of adventure pilgrimages having given up the drink before I found God again. But it was not the God of my Catholic upbringing but the God of my own understanding. A belief in the creative mind of my imagination. It was the Steps of AA that afforded me to be awakened to God again and hand over to him my life without reservation. For the next decade it all worked fine, that handing over and allowing God to work in and through me in helping other alcoholics achieve sobriety. However, something was missing. Whilst I was cynical about the logical linear half brain way of Catholic teaching then, leaning on the creative mind of belief in preference it all worked fine for a time. But I began to miss the structure of my former belief, especially the symbolism and signs of grace that the Mass and receiving the Eucharist (Holy Communion) in the service brought me. I began to visit a Church again, took time out to meditate in the quiet of the empty space there. Being more attentive to the meanings of all that exists within the bounds of any Church premise. In time I returned to Mass and found myself wanting to return to communion. I was in a loving relationship again with a Catholic lady who had lost her husband some years before and she too was in need of the solace of belief and love in our relationship. It was then my real dilemma began. According to the Canon Law of the Church, I was not welcome to participate in the communion ritual to receive the Eucharist, and because of being a divorced Catholic was not able to be married by a priest in the Church. Furthermore my new found love was (is) not able to receive communion either.

Surprisingly, in my previous life I had received all the Sacraments except Holy Orders which was reserved for those of priestly disposition. At one point in recovery after the marriage breakdown I had attended Mass whilst in hospital and it was a Mass for the Sick and without any further ado by the priest he administered the sacred oils on my forehead. So it was that I had received six of the seven Sacred Sacraments of the Holy Catholic Church, but now I was banned from two of them, namely the blessed receiving of the sacrament of Holy communion and marriage according to Church Law. In particular, I was no longer welcome to the fold of the Body of Christ Eucharist celebration. I had been married in the Church and now considered an outsider because I had been divorced and was in a relationship with a Catholic widow.

I was contemplating the contract of marriage in the Old and New Testaments and noted that like a contract for the buying and selling of animals, property, goods and services, the law of the times treated the marriage contract the same way with a point of difference. The contract and the ceremony of marriage within the Church, then and now stipulates an agreement that it's for a lifetime "until death do us part." But consider, until the early 20th century a lifetime was no more than 40 years of age. If someone made it beyond those years they were considered old. Today old age is more likely to be considered in the western world as being 60 years or beyond. People are living longer these days, so should those marriage contracts linked to Church laws still prevail in the light of old age and longevity? Whilst I have been divorced for two decades now, I am still kicking along at near age 80 years and with the grace of God will continue to do so for some time yet to come. Why should people who have grown apart in old age or one partner may be on death's door or in need of an aged care facility be forced to stay together. There are many who live under the same roof for convenience sake but do not live as married couples. I believe the church needs to have another look at its Canon law rule with regard to marriage, the receiving of the Eucharist and the right of other Christian faiths to participate in the Mass and receiving of the Eucharist host in that last supper reenactment celebration.

Until the day comes where the priest refuses me, as a divorced person, to participate in communion I will continue to trust in the God of my own understanding and his mercy. I will in good conscience and belief for the good of my soul, and the unity of the Body of Christ's people, continue to receive communion in the Mass celebration. I will continue to leave all judgment of my actions in this regard, not to the will of the priesthood, not to the written word of Canon Law, not to the Church itself, but to the Infinite Intelligence of the Father, Son and Holy Spirit in whom I trust. In further justification I turn to the ancient prayer of the Church acclaimed by the mystery of the Eucharist: "O sacred banquet in which Christ is received as food, the memory of his Passion renewed, the soul is filled with grace and a pledge of the life to come is given to us." If the Eucharist is the memorial of the Passover of the Lord Jesus, if by our communion at the altar we are filled with the heavenly grace," [Roman Missal Ep1, Canon Law 96) 'supplices te rogamus'] then the Eucharist is also an anticipation of then heavenly glory. For Jesus said: " I am the living bread that came down from heaven; if anyone eats of this bread, he will live forever;...he who eats my flesh and drinks my blood has eternal life and... abides in me, and I in him (James 6:51,54,56).

It is said in the catechism of the Catholic Church that the Eucharist is the heart and summit of the Church's life, for in it Christ associated his Church and all her members with his sacrifice of praise and thanksgiving offered once and for all on the cross to his Father; by this sacrifice he pours out by the grace of salvation on his Body which is the people, which is the Church. The celebration of the Eucharist proclaims the Word of God; in thanksgiving to God the Father for all his benefits, above all the gift of his Son; the consecration of bread and wine; and participation in the liturgical banquet by receiving the Lord's body and blood. These elements constitute one single act of worship. The memorial act of Christ passover, the work of salvation accomplished by his life, death and resurrection, a work made present by the liturgical action. It is Christ himself, the eternal high priest of the New Covenant who, acting through the ministry of priests, offers the Eucharistic sacrifice, and the same Christ, really present under the species of bread and wine, who is the offering of the Eucharistic sacrifice.

Now here is where my viewpoint on receiving the Eucharist of bread and wine as a renegade Catholic may well be taken to task in participating in the celebration of receiving communion from a priest at the Mass in contradiction of the Canon Law. I may well be considered a heretic in the eyes of the faithful Body of Christ who in their adhering to the rules of participation would frown down upon me with saintly reason in protest.For it is written that only validly ordained priests can preside at the Eucharist and consecrate the bread and wine so that they become the Body and Blood of the Lord.

The essential signs of the Eucharist sacrament are wheat bread and grape wine, on which the blessing of the Holy spirit is invoked and the priest pronounces the words of consecration spoken by Jesus during his Last supper: "This is my Body which will be given up for you…This is my blood." It is by the conversion of the substance of Eucharist elements into the body and blood of Christ at the consecration, only the appearance of bread and wine still remain. It is the essence of the spirit of Christ that then exists. It is considered then a living sacrifice that is offered in reparation for the sins of the living and the dead and to obtain spiritual or temporal benefit from God.

But in the view of the Church, anyone who desires to receive Christ in Eucharistic communion must be in a state of grace. Further, anyone aware of having sinned mortally must not receive communion without receiving absolution in the sacrament of penance. So if I take the view of the rule of Church doctrine as one who is divorced, as one who has a relationship with a woman who is not my legal wife, then in truth of the body of believers including the majority of priests, I cannot receive communion. Again, I take the view that I trust in the forgiveness of sin without the necessity of confession to a priest in-order to obtain forgiveness to receive the Eucharist. The priest himself consecrates the bread and wine and delivers it to the faithful but before doing so invites the assembly to participate: "Look not upon our sins but the Faith of the Church."i.e. the people assembled to partake of the host. "When we eat this bread and drink this wine, we proclaim your death O Lord, until you come again in glory.. Blessed are those called to the supper of the Lamb."

Assembly: "Lord, I am not worthy that you should enter under my roof, but only say the word and my soul shall be healed." I still stick to the firm belief that God forgives me in my honest attempt to receive him as the lifeblood of my time herein and in the world to come. Remembering the priest then announces: "Behold the Lamb of God, behold him who takes away the sins of the world. Blessed are those called to the supper of the Lamb." And the assembly of the Body of Christ responds: "Lord, I am not worthy that you should enter under my roof, but only say the word and my soul shall be healed." What more of a contrition is needed than that. Having parted from this world to the Father, Christ gives us his Eucharist with the pledge of glory with him. By participation in the Holy Sacrifice it identifies all his people with his Heart, sustains our strength along the pilgrimages of that life, make us long for eternal life, and unites us even now to the

Church in heaven, to the Blessed Virgin Mary and all the angels and saints. Be ye sinner or free in the sacraments of Christian initiation we receive a new life in Christ.

We carry in this earthly vessel what remains of a spirit soul which when being involved in the sacrifice of the Mass and the receiving of the Eucharist becomes "hidden with Christ in God" {[Corinthians 4: 7.} The priest administering the host says " The Body of Christ." and the participant in partaking of the host responds; "Amen," meaning " So may it be." When Christ's faithful strive to confess all their sins that they can remember, they undoubtedly place all of them before the divine mercy of God to be pardoned. In consideration of this, I am but a sick person trying to get well. In the fourth step of AA's 12 Step program we are helped to make courageous efforts to look at our life and identify negative thoughts, actions, and emotions that have led to or contributed to our addiction. In the 5th Step – We "Admitted to God, to ourselves, and to another human being the exact nature of our wrongs."

We can be alone at perfect peace and ease. Our fears fall from us. We begin to feel the nearness of our Creator. We may have had certain spiritual beliefs, but now we begin to have a spiritual experience. In so doing is this not a satisfactory contrition to follow up with being part and parcel of the Eucharist sacrifice without Church's doctrine of confessing one's sins to a priest in order to obtain forgiveness? So to be fair to the doctrine of the Credo in the Mass, despite my stubborn view of partaking of the host in my personal viewpoint, I am duty bound to take up the mantle and dissect the sacrament of healing, the one of penance and reconciliation.

It was my habit in my early adult life to keep up the practice of Sunday morning Mass. It was the Church's indoctrinated tradition to do so under pain of death, for it was considered a Mortal sin to not attend; a grievous offence against the laws of God. I, on this particular Sunday morning, was seated in the last pew near the entry of the narthex for a quick escape when the Mass had ended. I had already the habit of being there under sufferance but felt it my duty to attend despite my personal opinions or rebellion against the scaffold of religiosity that engulfed me. A long haired lout of the 60s did not fit the image of the well dressed congregation that Sunday morning.

CHAPTER 7.

PENANCE & RECONCILIATION

 Deep in thoughts of a philosophical kind, but conscious the Church was unusually full to the brim on this day, I was lost in my head space when the visiting priest left the altar after the initial traditional Mass prayers and slowly made his way to the pulpit. The Church attendees began to shuffle in their seats as he gazed down upon all in silence and surveyed with a prying eye, the Body of Christ's people. The silence continued for some time, then finally this pillar of the Church spoke out with a booming voice: "There is no such thing as sin." Well he certainly had my attention then.
The goodly friar of Franciscan order, like radical thinking with the brain of an Augustinian, began his sermon on the mountain of that pulpit. He raised his right hand and pointed his index finger squarely at the confessional box and shouted: "This is what's keeping good people from receiving the Eucharist." He then went on to preach the importance of accepting that our sins were removed by Christ's sacrifice on the cross. That we receive grace in the form of the Holy Spirit when we take in the holy host, the Body of Christ for our spiritual well being and that our current sin is washed away by his precious blood. " Father Frank, we shall call him here, for his animosity stop be continue to be protected from the conservatives within the Church to my way of thinking, despite that fact that the Church got its way with him in the long run, for he was ultimately relegated to a desk job in Perth, Western Australia, to keep his radical views at bay. On this day however, that little country church set its all time record for parishioners taking in the holiest of hosts in the Communion ritual. At the end of the Mass service that Sunday morning I quickly left the Body of the Church and entered the sacristy, where the priest   changed out of his vestments; the green robes in which he preached his long sermon. Father Frank greeted me with a typical Irish joviality and invited me to play a game of golf with him later in the day. I jumped at the chance to spend some one-on- one time with him, to pick his brains a little further as to his viewpoints, on belief and the practice of the Catholic faith in this embryonic time of change post Vatican 11.

  I quickly headed to my mother's home where I was staying for a few days. It had been an annual habit for me to visit my parent's home when on holidays and that was one of those occasions. Mum had been to an earlier Mass so she missed the radical priest's sermon. Perhaps it was ordained that way for she was one of very fixed black and white views when it came to her Catholic beliefs. I reckoned she would have fallen to her knees in silent prayer before one of the many statues of Mary that graced the rooms of the family home in gratitude that I was to meet up with the visiting priest, even if it was just going to play a game of golf. She would possibly have taken a back flip later, when the local Christian women's gossip group got together to mouth off about the visiting missionary priest's views on confession. Whilst Mum was a devout Catholic, my father didn't have much of a viewpoint for the likes of Church services, he was too busy building his material empire. I doubt if he even noticed the relics of Virgin Mother, Christ and the saints that adorned the wall of that little home. He did attend the Christmas midnight Mass service for the birth of Christ reenactment, and it was fortuitous that it was his birthday also. Dad told me that he always said his night prayers before falling asleep. Apart from that, in matters of faith he didn't much think about it but he was the most generous of men when it came to helping faiths of all kinds. He dug deep into his pockets to support all denominations, and equally donated monies to the Surf and Golf clubs. But I am getting away from the point here.

I learnt Father Frank had been a missionary priest in South Africa for many years. He told me during our golf match that it was his job to bring the Catholic faith to the native tribes and convert them to Catholicism. This he assured me was not what he ultimately did. For he had taken the view that they were more virtuous in their own traditional belief, more devoted than any Catholic doctrinal teaching would bring them too. We spoke a lot of their beliefs and the African native tribes sexual practices as opposed to our own puritanical one. He sighted the example of one tribe, where the elders selected their oldest sexually active man to teach the art of sex to young virgins. It was the duty of this man to take to the hills where he would teach each young virgin the art of sexual practice. The idea was that the young women, once having been trained in sexual intercourse by the elder, would know how to control the sudden urge of the young buck native they select to be the husband to procreate children with. I think I voiced the opinion at the time, the job of the elder far outweighed the newly wedded husband, who was locked into a relationship and family responsibility just to get his rocks off. The priest had laughed at this and he laughed even more when I told him that his story reminded me of the young bull laying on a hillside with the old bull, gazing down at the heifers in a nearby paddock. The young bull had remarked to the old one; " Let's trip down the hill quickly and grab one of those young heifers each and have our way with them." The old bull replied:' Let's stroll down slowly and do the lot."

Father Frank had commissioned me to do one last task for him before he ceased his religious zeal practice of travelling the country church to advice the flock to turn from their old style of belief & embrace the Eucharist by sidestepping the confessional box. He had a final stay with friends at Parramatta & asked if I would collect a 'gift of the spirit' for him sent from Ireland from a generous heart, or perhaps he had it on order in the ready, prior to his exit stage left to take up his new post in Perth in obedience to the College of Cardinals. Anyway I made my way to the Sydney docks Customs warehouse to collect his precious cargo. It turned out to be a couple of dozen bottles of the best Irish whisky. I loaded my boot with the nectar of the Gods to quench the thirst of any parched Irish throat & trotted off to a nearby bar to have a drink with an old friend I had prearranged to meet. To my great misfortune I got well into my cups & on my drive west to deliver the whisky to the patiently awaiting priest I had a horrific car accident almost writing off my car, causing irreparable damage to the one I collided with & and taking out a parked car in the process. Thankfully no one other than myself had been injured. I emerged from the hospital a day later with a shoulder injury and a sore hangover head.

God seemed to be on my side as the police took mercy upon me & I was not charged for driving under the influence, which was a great relief as it meant the insurance company would pay my claim and with a "no fault " clause in my policy they would pay for the other car's damage too. I ventured forth with my previous night's drinking mate to assess the damage to my car. The right hand front was almost unrecognisable and the boot had been flattened. Somehow as my car spun out of control down the road it took out a parked car too. With some operational effort we managed to pry open the boot with a crowbar, and miracle of miracles, not one bottle of whisky has been broken. The luck of the Irish I say or was it because God rewarded his own by his choosing, in particular a radical Irish priest who administered to his flock. He who in his had having encouraged so many Catholics around the country was soon circumvented by those of the left and sent off to whittle away his dotage as an administrator away from the flock. I lost track of Father Frank after he arrived in Perth, but in my wild erratic fancy sometimes pictured him with whisky in hand writing some litany of spiritual belief for those of us still radical Catholics to find and uncover in his philosophy. Or perhaps he returned to Ireland to follow the ways of St. Patrick, the Saint of the Isle! Either way I took a leaf out of his religious view in Mass participation, bypassing the confessional as he had so instructed. For I left the Church for a time, then after many years and tears I returned to religious practice, but I never forget the advice of that priest.

The memory of Fr. Frank reminded me of the zeal of Father Patton of the 1950s who also travelled the world encouraging devotion to the Virgin Mary by reciting the prayers of the Rosary and belief in the miracles of Fatima, where Mary reportedly appeared to three children requesting to pray the Rosary for the conversion of Russia whom she predicted would be the catalyst to peace in an ultimate Armageddon. Fr.Patton was the pioneer of mass marketers worldwide who's methodology in getting the word out there was successful long before the idea of social media was dreamt up. He could be heard on radio with the best of Hollywood actors at the time & had over a million regular American participants recite the Rosary prayers with him to quell the threat of Russia during those Cold War years. It may well be by his efforts both in the USA & internationally that stopped the war or indeed influenced world peace. Fr. Patton travelled the world financed by the CIA to promote his mission of prayer and peace. As a child, in the very same Church that Fr. Frank delivered his 'no sin' sermon, I heard Fr. Patton pray his mantra: "The family that prays together stays together. Rosary day, every day, in every family circle." My parents never encouraged that nor did they recite the rosary, but they stayed together anyway. In my own married life neither my then wife or I ever did encourage our children to pray the Rosary. More's the pity, for perhaps it could have saved the breakdown of our marriage.

Like Father Frank the Church ultimately grounded Fr. Patton by encouraging him to cease accepting funds for his travelling mission from the CIA. They obviously had their own agenda behind the scene, using Fr. Patton as a cover for what may well have been cloak and dagger deeds at the time. Who can be the judge of the CIA cause, for who knows what may have come down the pike had their intelligence service not been present around the world behind Patton's mission. It took another year of pressure by the Church's high rankers to convince Fr. Patton to cease his mission of accepting CIA funds for his cause. He was a celebrity by then, but was more than content in the end to bow out gracefully. So another Irish priest bit the dust at the bequest of Rome. But another out there Evangelist preacher soon took up the mantle of Father Patton on a world wide religious mission; his name was Billy Graham. And it is uncertain to this day if the CIA was or was not behind his mission also. It may be noted that I have no particular gripe with the work of the CIA in our troubled world. One can only hope and pray that the work they do in dark places will bring about peaceful solutions for the good of all. For evil can come from good deeds as equally as evil can result from badones. We must hope and pray that the CIA mission today is more for peaceful good purposes than that of will of the evil one.

As to my current day standard in the practice of the Faith I have had the occasion to obtain the viewpoint of a couple of other radical priests. One in relation to receiving communion, who gave me his advice in continuing to participate in the eating of the sacred Host without the necessary Church rule of confession to a priest first in order to obtain forgiveness of sin. And the other came from a Jesuit who was the priest who buried my son Peter. On seeking his advice about practicing my religious belief and having a relationship with a another woman but not being married to her, he said: "It's fine to have another woman in your life Doug, but that does not give you the freedom to shag every woman you meet." I hastened to add that whilst I took him at his word, it took quite a lot of holding the warm bodies of many damsels in distress before I found the one for whom I wished to remain true too and continue my religious practice.

As for the Church's teaching it would be unfair of me not to further state why the sacrament of penance is considered important. For it is the Church's opinion that Catholics must obtain pardon from Gods' mercy for the offences committed against Him. They also reconcile with the Church for the wounds that they have caused for their sins and which by charity, by example and prayer, have reconciled with forgiveness and the absolution administered by a priest in confession through renewing their conversion to the sacraments.. (This is of course is a Doug interpretation, but if one turns to Jesus in Matthew 5:14 he teaches that some things cannot be hidden and are simply not meant to be. Paul wrote that "believers can have their lives hidden with Christ in God in the sense that they do not have to conform to the carnality of this present world." (Colossians 3:3). This is a difficult one if taken literally. For it is called the sacrament of conversion because it makes the sacramentally present Jesus' call to conversion the first step in returning to The Father (Luke 15:18) from whom one had strayed by sin. It is also called the sacrament of Penance, since it consecrates the Christian sinner's personal and essential steps of conversion, penance, and satisfaction. Then it is also called the sacrament of confession, since the disclosure or confession of sins to a priest is an essential element of this sacrament. In a profound sense it is a "confession"-- if you will, an acknowledgement in praise of the holiness of God and the mercy towards sinful man. It is called the sacrament of forgiveness, since the priest's sacramental absolution God grants the penitent : "pardon and peace." Further, it is also called the sacrament of Reconciliation, because it imparts to the sinner the life of God who reconciles: " Be reconciled to God." (2 Cor 5:20.) He who lives by God's merciful love is ready to respond to the Lord's call: " Go, first be reconciled to your brother."(Matthew 5:24.) So it is said by the Church's teaching: "Individual, integral confession and absolution remain the 'only' ordinary way for the faithful to reconcile themselves with God and the Church, unless physical or 'moral impossibility' excuses from this kind of confession. There are profound reasons for this. Christ is at work in each of the sacraments. He personally addresses every sinner: " My son, your sins are forgiven." Mark 2:5 He is the physician tending each one of the sick who needs him to cure them. He raises them up and reintegrates them into fraternal communion. Personal confession is thus the form most expressive of reconciliation with God and with the Church. In brief, to return to communion with God after having lost it through sin is a process born of the grace of God who is rich in mercy and concern for the salvation of men. One must ask for this precious gift for oneself and for others.

The movement of return to God, called conversion and repentance, entails sorrow and abhorrence of sins committed, and the firm purpose of sinning no more in the future. Conversion touches the past and the future and is nourished by hope in God's mercy. I searched in vain in my examination of the Canon law of the Church to find some justification in circumventing the need for the sacrament of reconciliation through a priestly absolution of my mortal sin, that grievous offence against the law of God, that would cleanse me to partake of the Body and Blood of Christ in the Sacrament of the Holy Eucharist in the Last Supper reenactment of the Mass. I found some relief in thinking of the words of those priestly radicals of my former life who found that it was justified for me to go to communion despite the fact that I was a divorced person and was in a new relationship That it all seemed fine to a degree with me, but now I was in relationship with a part time Catholic widow, who practices the faith spasmodically like me, and neither of us could see the point in our marriage being in our twilight years and in fact we did not live together all the time. But the Canon Law of the Church is quite clear on being absolved from Mortal Sin: Anyone aware of having committed a grave sin is obliged to refrain from receiving Communion without first obtaining absolution in the sacrament of Reconciliation. Once confessed the priest may pray over the penitent sinner: " I absolve you from your sin, in the name of the Father, The Son and the Holy Spirit." Then he may say something like : "May the Almighty and Merciful Lord grant you indulgence, absolution, and remission of your sins. Amen." Both of these can be omitted for a just reason.

The Eucharist is one of four sacraments that imparts the forgiveness of sins. The waters of baptism wash away all prior sins. Both sacraments of healing — reconciliation and anointing — also grant forgiveness. The sacrament of reconciliation grants the absolution of both mortal and venial sins, and it offers God's pardon and peace. And the instruction to the sacrament of anointing says, "If they have committed any sins, their sins will be forgiven them" (see Jas 5:15).

When we attend Mass, even if we have not committed a mortal sin, we still have blemishes on our souls, the venial sins that we have committed. Some of these sins may be smaller, others may be larger, but they offend God and alienate us from his son Jesus and the body of Christ, the Church. A person with venial sins is still in the state of grace, and he or she is not only eligible to receive holy Communion, but also is encouraged to receive holy Communion. Then, when we receive the Eucharist, "Holy Communion separates us from sin … the Eucharist cannot unite us to Christ without at the same time cleansing us from past sins" (Catechism of the Catholic Church, No. 1393). When Jesus comes to us in the Eucharist, he wipes away our venial sins (see No. 1394). Jesus made the Eucharist-forgiveness connection at the Last Supper when he took a cup of wine and said, "This is my blood … which will be shed on behalf of many for the forgiveness of sins" (Mt 26:28).

The first generation of Christians considered the gift of forgiveness in the Eucharist to be a foundational belief: "by his blood … [we have] the forgiveness of sins previously committed" (Rom 3:25); "the blood of … Jesus cleanses us of all sins" (1 Jn 1:7); and, "Jesus Christ … has freed us from our sins by his blood" (Rv 1:5). The teaching that sins are forgiven in the reception of the Eucharist is reaffirmed in other writings and the words of the liturgy. St. Thomas Aquinas (1225-1274) referred to the Eucharist in a homily on the feast of Corpus Christi saying, "No other sacrament has greater healing power; through it sins are purged away." Preface I of the Most Holy Eucharist in the Roman Missal says, "As we drink his blood that was poured out for us, we are washed clean."

It is important to make a distinction when it comes to the forgiveness granted through the reception of the Eucharist: venial sins are forgiven, but mortal sins are not. The Catechism states, "The Eucharist is not ordered to the forgiveness of mortal sins — that is proper to the sacrament of reconciliation" (Credo Law No. 1395). St. Paul explained the danger of receiving holy Communion when a person is separated from God and neighbour: "Whoever eats the bread or drinks the cup unworthily will have to answer for the body and blood of the Lord (1 Cor 11:27).

According to the Church Law, a person with a mortal sin is not in the state of grace, and the path to Holy Communion is to approach the sacrament of reconciliation first, receive sacramental absolution, be restored to the state of grace, reestablish full communion with the Church, and then receive holy Communion. When we receive the Eucharist, Jesus extends to us his love, compassion, mercy, healing grace, pardon and peace. He offers us a new beginning, strengthens us in the battle against future sin, and nourishes us to live a virtuous and holy life. So in my current relationship, I am still considered to be in a state of living in grievous offence against the laws of God. So I am not reconciled with God through confessions and absolution if I am still continuing in an-out-of marriage relationship. Even if we were to marry again without my former marriage being justifiably annulled by the Church, I am not reconciled by Canon Law and the Churches teachings on the matter.

Until I began my brainwave of the logical linear delving into the Catechism of belief post Vatican 11, I was quite content to follow the dictates of my conscious, attend Mass and Communion when it suited me, visualizing the manifested Jesus of my creative mind, and receive Holy Communion in the Mass celebration by firstly confess my immorality directly to God, not having the need in my manifested belief to confessing to a priest in order to receive absolution to be forgiven. I felt justified in handing over to the power of the Mass celebration when the priest announced: "Look not upon our sins but the Faith of the Church. i.e. the people of God. I had no qualms in reciting a mantra, as I marched off to receive the Eucharist: "Not my will but thine be done." But after a time the former teachings of my Catholic life and the need for a reconciliation of sorts began to disturb my spirit. I was reminded of my former shattered life when I had taken up the mantle of belief as outlined in the Steps of Alcoholics Anonymous:, summed up in The Big Book of AA, Chapter 5 "...But there is One who has all power- that One is God. May you find Him now! Half measures avail us nothing. We stood at the turning point. We asked His protection and care with complete abandon." So it was that I took up the suggested steps of the program of recovery from my alcoholism and dare I say, it led me back to God.

We admitted we were powerless over alcohol- that our lives had become unmanageable.

2. Came to believe that a power greater than ourselves could restore us to sanity.

3. Made a decision to turn our will and our lives over to the care of God as we understood Him.

4. Made a searching and fearless moral inventory of ourselves.

5. Admitted to God, to ourselves.,and to another human being the exact nature of our wrongs.

6. Were entirely ready to have God remove all these defects of character.

7. Humbly asked Him to remove our shortcomings.

\8. Made a list of persons we had harmed , and became willing to make to them all.

9. Made direct amends to such people wherever possibly, except when to do so would injure them or others.

10. Continued to take personal inventory and when we were wrong prompt admitted it.

11. Sort through prayer and meditation to improve our conscious contact with God as we understood Him, praying only for knowledge of his will for us and the power to carry that out.

12. Having had a spiritual awakening as a result of these steps, we tried to carry this message to alcoholics, and practice these principles in all our affairs. The Principles set down here are guides to progress. We claim spiritual progress rather than spiritual perfection. Our spiritual personal adventure makes clear three pertinent ideas. (a) That we were alcoholic and could not manage our own lives. (b) That probably no human power could have relieved our alcoholism and (c) That God could and would if He were sought.

So, it was that I swallowed and digested the truths that were revealed by the fellowship of my programme of recovery and God answered me in his slow work and after a very short time I was relieved of the problem of alcoholism. I no longer desired to drink, but in its place a spiritual truth that applies to this alcoholic began to take shape and I thirst for the sacrament of the Last Supper and now and again return to my former Faith, content in the fact that I could participate fully in its rituals and religious ceremonies. But now in this delving I find the Church Canon law considers me unworthy to partake of the host. I find myself returning to my creative imagination of the God for the manifest of my own understanding to float my spiritual boat.

It is my desire to continue to examine the Catholic Creed, in spite of the restrictions placed upon my views of reconciliation and the grievous offence that the Church judges me on, I will continue."If you forgive others their transgressions, your heavenly Father will forgive you" (Mt 6:14). Perhaps in my further delving into the marriage rules as it relates to acceptance under Canon Law, then I may get further insight into practicing my Catholic faith, or maybe it will lead me to acceptance from another Christian denomination where the rules are not so insular. Catholicism has taught that if a person's first marriage ended in divorce, God won't bless a second one. Many Protestant traditions hold that since there are biblically justifiable grounds for divorce, God can bless a second marriage.

According to the Church's Code of Canon Law, a couple may be forced to separate and seek a divorce when circumstances are such that they cause "serious danger of spirit or body to the spouse or the children, or otherwise render common life too hard" (cf. #1153.1). Divorced people are full members of the Church and are encouraged to participate in its activities. May a divorced Catholic receive Holy Communion? Yes. Divorced Catholics in good standing with the Church, who have not remarried or who have remarried following an annulment, may receive the sacraments.

Jesus tells us in Luke 20:34-35 that there is no marriage in heaven. Marriage is an earthly institution with a heavenly purpose. Marriage is a training ground wherein we cosmic youngsters learn about the love that has existed

from all eternity within the Holy Trinity. Its purpose is to train us to give up our selfish tendencies, to care for another as we would care for ourselves, to take our place in the Kingdom of God. Marriage is a foreshadowing of our eternal relationship with God and with one another. Marriage is a wonderful thing, but it is not a forever thing. Knowing and remembering that should deepen not only the relationship with your earthly spouse, but also your love for your heavenly spouse, Jesus.

As a divorced Catholic I have taken great comfort from the story of Jesus' encounter with the woman of Samaria at Jacob's well (John 4:4-42). This poor woman had been married five times and was now living with yet another man. That's a lot of failed relationships—even by today's standards! Jesus' tenderness toward her and his sympathy for her situation are apparent. Did he deliberately go to that spot at that unlikely time of day because he knew she would be drawing water then? Did he send the disciples away to get lunch in the town so he could talk to her alone? I don't doubt it. Jesus never spoke to this woman or any other hurting person in ways that increased their pain. He offered this divorcee "living water, " himself, which was what she had been searching for in all her relationships. In my humble opinion it is time for the rest of the Catholic Church to do the same. The first thing Catholics should know is that divorce is not a sin that should keep a divorced Catholic from receiving the sacraments. A divorced or separated person is not excommunicated and is still a Catholic in good standing. The only reason for excommunication after divorce is remarriage without going through the annulment process. Before a divorced person can remarry in the Catholic Church, he or she must obtain an annulment by a Catholic diocesan tribunal. Obtaining such a decree does not mean that the marriage never took place; it is a determination that a sacramental marriage did not take place. This does not mean that the children of that marriage are illegitimate or that the couple was "living in sin. " It means that, in that particular case, the marrying couple had little or no idea what Christian marriage was all about or that there were deep problems from the beginning of the marriage, either in the couple's relationship or in their families of origin. Therefore, the Church may determine that it was impossible then for the couple to enter into a truly Christian marriage. Divorced Catholics who are seeking an annulment should talk to their pastors, who will direct them to the proper contacts at their diocese.

A divorce is a civil decree by which a marriage that existed has ended and is now dissolved. An annulment, on the other hand, is not a dissolution. It is an official declaration by a Church Tribunal that at the beginning of the marriage, the time of consent, something essential was lacking that pre
vented a marriage bond as understood by the Church, from coming into existence.

In Catholic law it is presumed that on their wedding day a couple were free and had the capacity to marry. Therefore, the basis for an annulment is the finding by the Tribunal that one or both parties in fact lacked something essential to consent to marriage, as understood by the Catholic Church. The essential elements for valid consent concern the knowledge, intentions, freedom and capacity of a person to undertake the obligations of marriage. There are a range of grounds under which an annulment can be applied for. For example, if at the time of consent one of the parties was under extreme pressure to marry, never intended to have children or during the ceremony was under the influence of drugs or alcohol. Tribunal personnel will be able to advise applicants if any grounds to challenge the validity of the marriage are suitable following an interview. In

practical terms, if a marriage is declared null, the Church considers the parties free of the marriage bond that would have otherwise arisen. The parties are then free to marry in the Catholic Church. Any divorced person has the right to ask for an investigation of a previous marriage by the Marriage Tribunal. Only a party to the marriage may apply. So one may ask, is it really worthwhile going through the tribunal process? And why do it, if one feels justified anyway in one's own acceptance of the participation in the sacrifice of the Mass and the receiving of communion? If one believes he/she is truly forgiven by God anyway, is it all worthwhile ? Well the process itself may be an experience of healing as an opportunity to reflect on the reasons for the breakdown of the previous relationship, develop greater understanding and a sense of closure. Whether a decree of nullity be issued or not, the decision for the peace of mind of this renegade Catholic will for the present remain and as a matter of faith in choosing to participate in the Mass and communion celebration despite the moral rule of confession to a priest to receive absolution before partaking in the reenactment of the last supper. However, in consideration of my Credo a more in depth look into The Church teaching on marriage is a worthy task.

CHAPTER 8.

THE SACRAMENT OF MATRIMONY

The marriage covenant, by which a man and a woman establish between themselves a partnership of their whole life, and which of its own very nature is ordered to the well-being of the spouses and to the procreation and upbringing of children, has, between the baptized, been raised by Christ the Lord to the dignity of a sacrament. [Canon Law 1055.]

It was in God's plan all along right from the start. Sacred Scripture begins with the creation of man and woman in the image and likeness of God and concludes with the '"wedding feast of the Lamb." [Revelations 19:7 and Genesis 1:26-27] Scripture speaks throughout of marriage and the "mystery," in its institution and the meaning God has given it, its origin and its end, its various realizations throughout the history of salvation, the difficulties arising from sin and its renewal "in the Lord" in the New Covenant of Christ and the Church. [1 Cor. 7:39]. So marriage according to biblical teachings and the Church has been established by the Creator and endowed by him with its own proper Laws. The vocation (Sacrament) of marriage is written in the very nature of man and women as from the hand of the Creator.

It is not a man made institution despite the many variations it has undergone through the centuries in different cultures, social structures and spiritual attitudes. We should not forget its common and permanent characteristics. The wellbeing of individual persons of both human and Christian society is closely bound up with a healthy state of conjugal and family life. At least that seems to have been God's plan. Consider, God created man out of love and also called him to love- It is the fundamental and innate vocation of every human being. For in all of the magic and mystery of life, he created man in his own image and likeness. God who himself is love, gave man a woman to love and in turn has expectations for us to love all and him back for the gift of eternal love. "And God blessed them, and God said to them: Be fruitful and multiply, and fill the earth and subdue it," (Gen 1:28).

Holy Scripture affirms that man and woman were created for one another: " It is not good that man should be alone." (Gen 2:18) God had considered from the beginning that they would be an unbreakable union for " a lifetime." God had created in the beginning; "So they are no longer two but one flesh." (Matthew 19:6).

Then cometh the experience of evil that lay within the heart of every man. This experience makes itself felt in the relationship between man and woman.Their union has always been threatened by discord ever since Eve tempted Adam with the forbidden fruit encouraged by that snake,Satan, or however you may perceive it to be. That discord of divide and rule was, and still is, a satanic way of turning mankind from light to darkness, or from good to evil if you will. In marriage it comes in a spirit of domination, infidelity, jealousy, and conflict that can escalate into hatred and separation. This discord can manifest itself more or less acutely, and can more or less be overcome according to the circumstances of the culture, era, and individuals, but it does seem to have a universal character.

According to faith the discord we notice so painfully does not stem from the nature of man and woman, nor from the nature of their relationship but it does come from wrongdoing, intentional mistakes that religion calls sin which I prefer to define as defects of character. It is a break with the God of our own understanding, as the Bible defines. It was, and is, a rupture from inception of the original communion between man and woman. [Their relations were distorted by mutual recriminations. Genesis 3:12 Their mutual attraction changed into a relationship of domination and lust. Genesis 2:22]. So the plan of a beautiful sacred vocation of man and women to be fruitful, multiply, and subdue the earth was burdened by the pain of childbirth and the toil of work.

Nevertheless, the order of creation persists, through serious disturbance, both in man and in nature. The Church teaches that to heal the wound of wrongdoing, man and woman need the grace of God in his infinite mercy which he never refuses them. Without his help man and woman cannot achieve the union of their lives for which God created them in the beginning.

In the Old Testament, the polygamy practice of having more than one wife or husband at the same time, of the male head of a tribe, biblical figures of the human race, or kings and bishops of the most ancient Christian tribes, was not explicitly rejected. Then along came Moses who determined the law via the Commandments given to him by God at the event of the burning bush. When it came to interpretation of the marriage rule Moses aimed to protect the wife from arbitrary dominion by the husband, knowing the Lord's words in the traces of man's hardness of heart in such matters. And this is why Moses permitted men to divorce their wives.

So it was in Bible speak [seeing God's covenant with Israel in the image of exclusive and faithful married love, the prophets prepared the Chosen People's conscience for a deepened understanding of the unity and "indissolubility friendship" of marriage.] (Isa. 54;62, Esek 16; Matthew 2:13-17) Henceforth throughout the Bible there are stories bearing witness to an elevated sense of marriage and the fidelity and tenderness of spouses. In the song of Solomon there is a unique expression of human love, and a pure reflection of God's love, a love as "strong as death" that then "many waters cannot quench." Song 8:6-7.Fast forwarded from the Old testament to the New Testament, there the nuptial covenant between God and his people Israel had prepared the way for a new and everlasting covenant in which Jesus, the son of God, by becoming incarnate and giving his life, has united himself in a certain way that all mankind is saved by him, thus preparing for "the wedding of the lamb." Revelations 19:7.

On the threshold of his public life Jesus performs his first sign- at his mother's request- during a wedding feast. John 2:1-11. Catholic Church teachings attach great importance to Jesus' presence at the wedding at Cana. Mother Church sees in the confirmation of the goodness of marriage and the proclamation that the henceforth marriage will be a beneficial sign of Christ's presence. In his teachings Jesus unequivocally taught the original meaning of the union of man and women as the Creator ordained from the beginning: that the mission given by Moses to divorce one's wife was a concession to the 'hardness of hearts' of man. (Matthew 19:8.)

Jesus, by coming to restore the original order of creation disturbed by man's defects of character, he himself gives strength and grace to live marriage in the new dimension of the Reign of God. It is by following Christ, renouncing themselves, and taking up the crosses that spouses will be able to "receive" the original meaning of marriage and live it with the help of Christ. Matthew 19:11 This grace of Christian marriage is a fruit of Christ's cross, the source of all Christian life. A communion of the Body and Blood of Christ in the sacrifice of the Mass. A reenactment of the Last Supper, of Christ sacrifice on the cross, to partake of the host of the grace of God, to wipe away the wrongdoings of man and save us from ourselves. It is by following Christ, renouncing ourselves, talking up the crosses that marriage is burdened with, that we are able to receive the original meaning of the union and live with the help of Christ. The grace of Christian marriage is a fruit of Christ's cross, the source of all Christian life, 'irrespective of one's present circumstance.' [Doug speak]

Christ is the centre of Christian life. The bond with him takes precedence over all other bonds, familiar or social.(Mark 10:28-31 Luke 14:26.) From the very beginning of the Church there have been men and women who have renounced the great good of marriage to follow The Lamb of God wherever he goes, to be intent on the things of the Lord, to seek to please him, and to go out to meet the Bridegroom who is coming. (Revelation 14:4.) These souls have renounced the world in preference to be the guiding force for the doctrines of faith and morals, as it applies to the people, especially in marriages. It is the Church's teaching that the virginity for the sake of the kingdom of heaven is an unfolding of baptismal grace, a powerful sign of the supremacy of the bond with Christ and the ardent expectation of his return, a sign which also recalls that marriage is a reality of this present age which is passing away.

What appears good only in comparison with evil would not be truly good. The most excellent good is something even better than what is admitted to be good. For a marriage to be valid there arises a bond between the spouses which by their very nature is perpetual and exclusive. Furthermore, in a Christian marriage the spouses are strengthened and, as it were, consecrated for the duties and dignity of their state by a special sacrament (Mark 10:9)

The consent by which the spouses mutually give and receive one another is sealed by God himself (Mark 10.9) From covenant arises "an institution, conformed by divine law,...and even by the eyes of society." The covenant between spouses is integrated into God's covenant with man "Authentic married love is caught up in divine love," [Gaudium et spes 48; as qualified by divine law according the Vatican 11] It is this belief that the marriage bond has been established by God himself in such a way that a marriage once concluded and consummated between two baptized persons can never be dissolved. This bond, which results from the free human act of the spouses and their consummation of the marriage is a reality henceforth irrevocable, and gives rise to a covenant guaranteed by God's fidelity. The Church does not have the power to contravene this disposition of divine wisdom. [Canon law 1141]

The dissolving of a marriage through divorce is frowned upon to this day and has current barriers for intended spouses of a second marriage without a bona fide case for an **annulment**. Pope Francis has though made it easier, quicker and free for Catholics to have their marriages annulled under reforms conservatives fear may lead to church-approved divorce. Details of changes to a system that critics, including Pope Francis himself, had attacked as needlessly bureaucratic, expensive and unfair were unveiled. A papal letter was published on the issue and released to Catholic churches across the world.(September 2015). The title of the document was "Mitis Iudex Dominus Iesus", Latin for "The Lord Jesus, the Gentile Judge".

In it, the Argentinian Pontiff said annulments would henceforth require only one decision rather than having to be approved by two church tribunals. An annulment, formally known as a "decree of nullity", is a ruling that a marriage was not valid in the first place according to church law because certain prerequisites, such as free will, psychological maturity and openness to having children, were lacking. A streamlined procedure was introduced with most cases to be handled by individual bishops rather than subject to a hearings process. Appeals to a Vatican court against individual annulments will still be possible but will become the exception not the rule. The Pope's letter follows a year-long review by experts in religious law. It also asks bishops conferences to ensure there are no costs involved in the process of securing an annulment. While

Pope Francis is seeking to democratize the procedure in a way that would appear to make an increase in the number of annulments likely, his letter does not amend the exceptional conditions under which they can be granted. In his letter, he strongly reaffirms the principle of the indissolubility of marriage while highlighting the "enormous number of believers" for whom annulment is currently not an option for various reasons.

Although the notion of marriage being for life is one of the fundamental tenets of the Catholic faith, divorce has become commonplace among believers across much of the industrialized world. Church doctrine allows for unions to be canceled — effectively declared to have never existed — when the marriage is judged to have been fundamentally flawed from the outset. Possible justifications for reaching this conclusion include non-consummation of the marriage, one or both partners having entered into it without the intention of staying in the relationship, or one of the partners having no desire to have children. Alcohol and drug dependency can also be taken into consideration. In practice, access to the annulment procedure currently varies widely. There is virtually no provision for it in many dioceses in the developing world while many ordinary Catholics in wealthier countries simply do not understand the complex procedures or cannot afford expert legal help to guide them through the processes.

[So like all things in Canon Law, in spite of the changes proposed by the Pope, it is a trust in the slow work of God where renegade Catholics who still seek to practice their faith and receive the sacraments of Holy Communion are considered in a state of mortal sin and are doing so against the Laws of God. The yet to be proven relaxed rules for annulment are a breath of fresh air for renegade Catholics such as myself. Current Canon Law is not just antiquated when it comes to marriage annulment or acceptance of new relationships, but is judging the agreement of the marriage bond by former days when people were considered in old age at 40 years. Now, it is not so uncommon to have divorced people living to their late 60s and early 90s.] Doug Speak [.Is it fair to those people with today's longevity to be punished by outdated Canon Law and the marriage agreement as it now stands?]

Equally is it justifiable that one must confess one's 'sins' to a priest, to be absolved in order to participate in receiving the communion host of Christ in the Mass celebration? There are many examples throughout biblical reference where it seems justified. Further, other Christian religious denominations have a much more inviting and acceptable view for those of us left in the dark of our own conscious thoughts regarding the rules of forgiveness in the Catholic faith. This is a personal opinion I am stating here and in which I stand by and stand corrected if it proves to me to be contrary to my current relationship, and my belief in receiving the sacraments within the Church. My present belief I leave to the power granted to me by the God of my own understanding, faith in the risen Christ and the grace bestowed upon me through the Holy Spirit to judge me on my belief that I am granted God's blessing to "Look not on my sins but the faith of his Church," the body of the congregation who receive the host, that is those who are the communion of saints who believe in the divine mercy of the Trinity.

Listening to the word of God seems to be the key to all spiritual learning. Attending the sacrifice of the Mass, perseverance in prayer, and the continuance in working for the benefit of others, to give and not to count the cost, working for the benefit of the community or group, for justice, for family, for children in a Christian manner. To cultivate the spirit and practice of a personal penance to God is the ideal to cultivate for all these reasons, but in reality?

In our time, in a world that is often alien and even hostile to faith, the family unit has broken down. The central mission of the Church has always had at its core the family as central to living radiant faith. The Second Vatican Council used an ancient expression, calling the family "Ecclesia domestica"…the bosom of the family by parents as by word and example… the first heralds of faith with regard to their children. It is here that all family members exercise the privilege of their Catholic baptism "by the reception of the sacraments, prayer and thanksgiving, the witness of the holy life, and self-denial and active charity." This in detail was expressed in Vatican 11 in great details as 'Gaudium et spes' is a worthy read as an expression of faith and mission for an ideal world, but nevertheless should be considered as we head ever more closely to a One World Government with a singular agenda of control by the Elite class, but don't get me started on that. Here in detail is Gaudium Et spes: [Through his labours and his native endowments man has ceaselessly striven to better his life. Today, however, especially with the help of science and technology, he has extended his mastery over nearly the whole of nature and continues to do so. Thanks to increased opportunities for many kinds of social contact among nations, the human family is gradually recognizing that it comprises a single world community and is making itself so. Hence many benefits once looked for, especially from heavenly powers, man has now enterprisingly procured for himself.

In the face of these immense efforts which already preoccupy the whole human race, men agitate numerous questions among themselves. What is the meaning and value of this feverish activity? How should all these things be used? To the achievement of what goal are the strivings of individuals and societies heading? The Church guards the heritage of God's word and draws from its moral and religious principles without always having at hand the solution to particular problems. As such she desires to add the light of revealed truth to mankind's store of experience, so that the path which humanity has taken in recent times will not be a dark one.

Throughout the course of the centuries, men have laboured to better the circumstances of their lives through a monumental amount of individual and collective effort. To believers, this point is settled: considered in itself, this human activity accords with God's will. For man, created to God's image, received a mandate to subject to himself the earth and all it contains, and to govern the world with justice and holiness;(1) a mandate to relate himself and the totality of things to Him Who was to be acknowledged as the Lord and Creator of all. Thus, by the subjection of all things to man, the name of God would be wonderful in all the earth.(2)This mandate concerns the whole of everyday activity as well. For while providing the substance of life for themselves and their families, men and women are performing their activities in a way which appropriately benefits society. They can justly consider that by their labor they are unfolding the Creator's work, consulting the advantages of their brother men, and are contributing by their personal industry to the realization in history of the divine plan.(3)

Thus, far from thinking that works produced by man's own talent and energy are in opposition to God's power, and that the rational creature exists as a kind of rival to the Creator, Christians are convinced that the triumphs of the human race are a sign of God's grace and the flowering of His own mysterious design. For the greater man's power becomes, the farther his individual and community responsibility extends. Hence it is clear that men are not deterred by the Christian message from building up the world, or impelled to neglect the welfare of their fellows, but that they are rather more stringently bound to do these very things.(4) Human activity, to be sure, takes its significance from its relationship to man. Just as it proceeds from man, so it is ordered toward man. For when a man works he not only alters things and society, he develops himself as well. He learns much, he cultivates his resources, he goes outside of himself and beyond himself. Rightly understood this kind of growth is of greater value than any external riches which can be garnered. A man is more precious for what he is than for what he has.(5) Similarly, all that men do to obtain greater justice, wider brotherhood, a more humane disposition of social relationships has greater worth than technical advances. For these advances can supply the material for human progress, but of themselves alone they can never actually bring it about.Hence, the norm of human activity is this: that in accord with the divine plan and will, it harmonizes with the genuine good of the human race, and that it allows men as individuals and as members of society to pursue their total vocation and fulfil it.

Now many of our contemporaries seem to fear that a closer bond between human activity and religion will work against the independence of men, or of the world at large. If by the autonomy of earthly affairs we mean that created things and societies themselves enjoy their own laws and values which must be gradually deciphered, put to use, and regulated by men, then it is entirely right to demand that autonomy. Such is not merely required by modern man, but harmonizes also with the will of the Creator. For by the very circumstance of their having been created, all things are endowed with their own stability, truth, goodness, proper laws and order. Man must respect these as he isolates them by the appropriate methods of the individual sciences or arts. Therefore if methodical investigation within every branch of learning is carried out in a genuinely scientific manner and in accord with moral norms, it never truly conflicts with faith, for earthly matters and the concerns of faith derive from the same God. (6) Indeed whoever labours to penetrate the secrets of reality with a humble and steady mind, even though he is unaware of the fact, is nevertheless being led by the hand of God, who holds all things in existence, and gives them their identity. Consequently, we cannot but deplore certain habits of mind, which are sometimes found too among Christians, which do not sufficiently attend to the rightful independence of science and which, from the arguments and controversies they spark, lead many minds to conclude that faith and science are mutually opposed.(7) But if the expression, the independence of temporal affairs, is taken to mean that created things do not depend on God, and that man can use them without any reference to their Creator, anyone who acknowledges God will see how false such a meaning is. For without the Creator the creature would disappear. For their part, however, all believers of whatever religion always hear His revealing voice in the discourse of creatures. When God is forgotten, however, the creature itself grows unintelligible.

I was reflecting on the fact that I have always bucked the system in favour of my own rules. In my youth I bent the rules of family, school, the Church and community. This often caused me pain and sorrow. I really don't like being ruled. If I consider consciously Canon Law in relation to my present life, bending the rules in my favour comes naturally to me. It seems the Church does not allow for any shade of grey in its teachings. To me spiritual life is not like their rule of law in relating to reconciliation, marriage and receiving the Eucharist in the Mass celebration. In this I still remain the renegade.

Jesus was only twelve when he found the rules hard to take, he broke loose and left home without notice teaching the priests in the Temple the right way to interpret the doctrines of faith and moral in accord the Torah and not their own. Jesus set himself free even from family. He had to be himself in being about his fathers business. Eventually Jesus accept the wisdom of Mary and Joseph, and went back with them to Nazareth, there to grow under their guidance into the real man that it was his heavenly Father's will to become. I suppose the really important thing is that I never lose my desire to grow, to be my real self, to be free, and yet to still accept the rules you have chosen for me.

CHAPTER 9.

ANCIENT MYTHS AND CULTURAL NORMS

In the light of a personal credo for living a spiritually fruitful life today, I began to reexamine and reevaluate the recorded context of Canon Law of the Church, those laws as they apply to man's nature and society at large. I was thinking of my former indoctrination to a rote-like learning of The Christian Bible; the Old Testament and the New Testament. I recalled that The Old Testament was (is) from the original Hebrew Bible, the sacred scriptures of the Jewish faith, written at different times between about 1200 and 165 BC. The Catholic faith back in my upbringing paid scant focus on the ways of that teaching , except to make a point or two in the coming of the Saviour in keeping with the The New Testament in the form of the Catechism of the Catholic faith, all centred on the birth, death and resurrection of Jesus. How he came to give himself up in sacrifice so that we may be free from the slavery of sin and live life according to the commandments. I recalled that the New Testament books were written by Christian saints in the first century AD.

There is evidence that shows that the four Gospels were written in a relatively short time after the death and resurrection of Jesus Christ. Examining the internal evidence of the New Testament itself can make this plain. The evidence is as follows: 1. The City of Jerusalem and the Temple were still standing when the gospels were written. The first three Gospels, and possibly also the fourth, were apparently written while the city of Jerusalem was still standing. Each of the first three Gospels contains predictions by Jesus concerning the destruction of Jerusalem and the Temple (Matthew 24; Mark 13; Luke 21), but none records the fulfilment. We know that Titus the Roman destroyed the city and Temple in A.D. 70. Hence, the composition of the first three Gospels most likely occurred sometime before this event, otherwise their destruction would have been recorded. The fact that all four gospels are written from the perspective that the city of Jerusalem and the temple had not been destroyed gives evidence of an early date. 2. The Book of Acts also provides us with a clue as to when the gospels were written. Acts records the highlights in the life and ministry of the Apostle Paul. The book concludes with Paul at Rome awaiting trial before Caesar. It says: And Paul dwelt two whole years in his own hired house, and received all that came in unto him, preaching the kingdom of God, and teaching those things which concern the Lord Jesus Christ, with all confidence, no man forbidding him. (Acts 28:30-31). The New Living Translation reads:

For the next two years, Paul lived in his own rented house. He welcomed all who visited him, proclaiming the Kingdom of God with all boldness and teaching about the Lord Jesus Christ. And no one tried to stop him. The inference is that Acts was written while Paul was still alive, seeing that his death is not recorded. Since there is good evidence that Paul died in the Neronian persecution about A.D. 67, the Book of Acts can be dated approximately A.D. 62. 3. Luke's Gospel Was Written Earlier than Acts.

If Acts was written about A.D. 62, then this helps us date the four gospels. The Book of Acts is the second half of a treatise written by Luke to a man named Theophilus. Since we know that the Gospel of Luke was written before the Book of Acts, we can then date the Gospel of Luke sometime around A.D. 60 or before. 4. The Brother Who Was Well-Known May Have Been Luke. There may be further evidence for an early date for Luke's gospel. Paul wrote of a brother who was well-known among the churches for the gospel: And we are sending along with him the brother who is praised by all the churches for his service to the gospel.(2 Corinthians 8:18) There is ancient testimony that this refers to Luke and his written gospel. If this is speaking of Luke and the gospel he composed, then we have it well-known in the mid-fifties of the first century.5. Mark may have been a source for Luke.

There may be a reference in the writings of Luke that he used Mark as a written source. John Mark is called a "minister" by Luke in Acts 13:5 (the Greek word huparetas). In 1:2, Luke says he derived the information for his gospel from those who were "eyewitnesses" and "ministers" of the word. The term translated "minister" is the same Greek word huparetas. It is possible that this could be a reference to Mark as one of his written sources. 6. Mark Was Likely Written Before Luke. Furthermore, modern scholarship has generally assumed that the Gospel of Mark was written before Luke. If this is the case, then we are somewhere in the fifties of the first century when this book was composed. Since Jesus' death and resurrection occurred approximately in the year A.D. 33, these two gospels were written during the time when eyewitnesses, both friendly and unfriendly, were still alive. These eyewitnesses could either verify or falsify the information contained in the gospels. 7. Matthew was always believed to have been written first. We now go a step further by considering Matthew's gospel. According to the unanimous testimony of the early church, Matthew was the first gospel written. The church father Eusebius places the date of Matthew's gospel in A.D. 41. If the ancient testimony is true, and there is no reason to doubt it, then we have a third independent source about the life of Christ written during the eyewitness period. 8. John was an Eyewitness to the Events. The Gospel of John is usually assumed to have been the last of the four gospels composed. John testified that he was an eyewitness to the events that he recorded. He said:Now Jesus did many other signs in the presence of the disciples, which are not written in this book; but these are written so that you may believe that Jesus is the Christ, the Son of God, and that by believing you may have life in his name. (John 20: 30-31)

The *New Living Translation* puts it this way: Jesus' disciples saw him do many other miraculous signs besides the ones recorded in this book. But these are written so that you may believe that Jesus is the Messiah, the Son of God, and that by believing in him you will have life. John also wrote: "This is the disciple who is bearing witness about these things, and who has written these things, and we know that his testimony is true." (John 21:24). It is clear that John claimed to have been there when the events in the life of Jesus transpired.

There is also internal evidence that John himself wrote before A.D. 70. We read the following description of Jerusalem in the fifth chapter of John: Now there is in Jerusalem by the "Sheep Gate" a pool called Bethesda in Aramaic, which has five covered walkways. John 5:2): John describes the sheep gate as still standing at the time he wrote. He could not have made this statement after A.D. 70—there was no sheep gate. The sheep gate was destroyed in the year A.D. 70, along with the rest of the city of Jerusalem. This could very well be an indication that John wrote his gospel before the city of Jerusalem was destroyed.

Conclusion: There Is evidence for an early date for the four Gospels.
When all the historical and textual evidence is amassed, it becomes clear that the four gospels were composed at a very early date either by eyewitnesses, or those who recorded eyewitness testimony. Therefore, we have every reason to trust what they wrote.
So why am I bothering to show verification of the Gospels when I have already provided enough evidence in a previous chapter that Christ walked the earth, recruited Apostles and disciples to follow him and to "go out and preach to all nations his message of salvation? To pray to God as in the Sermon on the mountain. "To eat his flesh and drink his blood" in commemoration of him as he requested at the last supper before he suffered death on the cross for the sins of humanity, and ascended into heaven?
Well, it's more from the point of difference that long before the Old Testament or the New testament were written man walked the earth. So what of those people millions of years before Christ story, before the Vatican existed, before the creeds of faith were written down like a mission statement for mankind to follow, what happened back there for mankind to believe in ?
I had been discussing the aspects of the existence of man in the pre Christian times with a Portuguese friend whom I met in Lisbon city before I tramped my weary way on my second Camino de Santiago in 2015. I was there on a follow-up mission to find recorded evidence of a Portuguese Caravel ship that wrecked off the coast of Victoria during the Spice Age of the 15th century. Spices were a major motivating factor in the European Age of Exploration then, when the search for direct access to the highly lucrative Eastern spice trade began. The exploration via the Middle East land and sea routes from the Indian coastline to as far away as Indonesia, yielded spices in huge demand both for food dishes and for use in medicines.It was a good excuse for me to check out Portuguese

Europe at the time. I was keen to find records of the background to the wreck and why it had been in Australian waters at the time. It was not the only reason I was walking another Camino. There were stories of an apparition of the Virgin Mary on the coastline not far from Lisbon, and also that St.James had travelled to Portugal to preach the Gospel as he reportedly had done on the Camino Way, the route that I took 2013. I had my doubts that St. James ever preached in Spain or Portugal but I had been drawn to return to walk the French Route again in 2017. Records show that James' zeal for Jesus resulted in his being the first of the twelve apostles to be martyred. He was killed with the sword on order of King Herod Agrippa I, dying about 44 A.D. in a general persecution of the early church. My motivation to walk the Portuguese Camino was also motivated by the desire to explore Fatima on route, and the fact that my new acquaintance was keen to show me the sights off route of the Portuguese Camino Way made for much pleasantry for my adventurers.

The morning after my arrival in Lisbon, we wound our way up a maze of unmade lanes before climbing to a dusty track to a cork plantation at the peak of a hill near Evora. We alighted from my companions car to the site of Portugal's Stonehenge; some two thousand years older than the Wiltshire stone circle, the Cromlech of the Almendres stands. It is one of the largest megalithic sites in Europe and is perfectly positioned to celebrate the Solstice, as they do in Stonehenge. The last of the carpet of spring wildflowers were still on display and the sense of nature and man manifested in a sacred grove of stone. Standing amongst ninety huge granite stones, it felt like being in a corpulent crowd of granite friends, jostling to see something. I pictured the itinerant hunter-gatherers' transition to agriculture some 5000 years BC when these stones, by scientific verification, are reported to have been erected.

 What makes its astronomical orientation even more certain is the presence of two vast outriding stones marking the summer and the winter solstice.At the equinox in spring and autumn, both the sun and the moon would rise at the same point along the axis of the stones; a perfect methodology for budding crop growers to determine when to sow and reap the harvest. Nearby graves housed human bones, hunting and agricultural implements too. It seemed like they had human sacrifice to the Gods or paid homage by burying their dead at the site. The symbolic stones were not only an astronomical guidance method to the tribe's survival, but a modern day reminder of their very existence. As I thought back to this, the second of my Camino's, I was reminded of the news in the local papers prior to leaving home of an Indigenous rock shelter near Kakadu that pushes Australia's human history back 65,000 years, up to 18,000 years earlier than any archaeologists previously believed. My homeland of ancient wisdom and this hallowed land on the Iberian Peninsula, with an even more bloody history than that of my own, speaks to me of savagery, poverty, power, prestige, kingdoms of conquest, social uprising, defeat and heroism. Endless circles of action and reaction flows on even to the present. The hallowed earth in which I then stood, foreshadowed by the ancient Iberian Peninsula monuments, a testament to the tribes that evolved throughout the ages had left me silent and speechless. My sacred moment had added some colour to the large ancient stones that I was gazing upon back there in 2015.

Tracing backwards through the history of this foreign land, I was slowly coming to terms within my mind to an understanding of those ancient races of Homo Sapiens, back to the hunter gatherers transition to agricultural crop growing some 5000 years ago in Portugal and back also to the Australian Aboriginal hunter gatherers of 65,000 years ago. Those forgotten years dated far beyond the age of these ancient stones that I touched as they touched me spiritually. Here I was, a modern man in my Portuguese Camino, in the summer of 2015, recalling stories of the ancients before the Bible stories of good and evil and the New Testament gospels of the birth, death and resurrection of Christ. Well before all that I had been schooled in the the existence of these ancient people.. What did these great hunters and farmers believe in? Myth, legends and folklore that have provided man through the tests of time with reasons for living and hoping. Just as the Bible, the Torah and the Koran did later and do today for believers and to some degree non-believers.

My guide Luisa and I made our way to the Cape Sanctuary, where the origins of the cult of 'Our Lady of the Cape' began back in the 15th Century. The Church there, whilst abandoned except for the occasional tourist, is built in late classical style, following the model of Jesuit churches. The strikingly beautiful painting of Our Lady of the Assumption on small blue Portuguese tiles adorned the walls, still in original condition, having weathered the deterioration one would expect over the centuries. Panels of walls in blue tiles recalled legends of the Lady of The Cape, riding a mule whose foot marks are imprinted in stone later proven to be a myth. In reality, the footprints have been proven to be those of two dinosaurs. Another myth busted saw the decline of pilgrimages to the location that has left a beautiful locally hewed-stone church, where once traders sold their wares. We made our way back along a coastal route towards a sleepy fishing village where we planned to have a bite to eat, a cool drink and a relaxing walk along the beach.

As we walked, I got to thinking about man's need for a power greater than self. A dream, a myth or a reality; something to keep one's hopes alive, something to be motivated about from a spiritual aspect, something to live for. My Aboriginal brothers back in Australia certainly lived that way for thousands of years. It has traditionally been an Aboriginal belief that a culture of Gods travelled across a land without form and created sacred sites and significant places giving the language to a tribe of their people. The modern day Aboriginal still goes 'walk-about' into the dream time, still dances, still tells their stories in song lines and fights for traditional rights of land and spirituality. My mind drifted to the mythology that I too was conditioned to believe in-Christian myths, symbols and signs of my childhood that was painfully engraved into my being. Make-believe which still clings to me like scaffolding on an unfinished building project

Back home in Australia, I pictured the swamp oak trees of the Aboriginal song-lines sighing incessantly hungering for rain, the gum trees shedding tears of blood and turning into red gum. Bleeding as Christ had done in the Garden of Gethsemane, turning into dry blood on that Sacred face, his blue eyes tortured for what he could foresee, the future folly of mankind; wars and sufferings ahead and my then physical passion for this foreign maiden. I could not see it then, as I walked my second Camino. I could not see it as I walked this third Camino, looking back on the first and the second one. As I write these lines, I see it now- the sad conclusion of the hopes of the Aboriginal peoples, the hopes of the world today, black or white, the folly of an old Camino man, walking in a strange land, looking to the sky and thinking of my homeland of the Southern Cross and of all of mankind's beginnings in Africa. We are all descendants of the Dreaming, be we black, white or brindle.

The Dreaming

Gary the Elder made his way to the old Coolabah tree not far from the great rock known as Uluru and sat in the shade of a tree. Eucalyptus leaves above his head haunting the ghost-like branches. He lay his back against the rough tree trunk and waited for the children in the twilight of the evening, as he watched the last ray of sunlight fade beyond the horizon. It was at the same daily time at twilight that he ventured to sit by the tree awaiting the children of the current generation to come, to sit at his feet. He was there to teach old ways of dreaming and stories of the song lines. Gary glanced at the surrounding desert plain, gazing at the light and shadows reflected on the great rock ring some high distance away. It seems larger now in the afternoon light, the great pebble in the desert shining bright red across various shades of Orchha, like the desert surrounds. The view of the red Rock of Ulura held great spiritual significance to Gary the elder and his ancestors. It was to their mind created at the beginning of time, known as the dreamtime; when the natural environment was born and the dreamtime spirits came up from earth and down from the sky to walk over this barren land creating shape and life forms with animals and man, altering the natural landscape to perform sacred rituals in the dreaming and song lines stories handed down to the tribes to tell the coming generation. To his reckoning there were always elders of the tribe to teach the old ways and now it was his turn.

It seems like only yesterday to me that my classmate of education with those Irish nuns had taught us, both black and white and no shades of gray, the Christian principle of God, the Trinity and what was considered good moral virtue. Gary had been a class below me, so he was a year younger, but we both played for the school in the local Rugby League inter-schools competition. We were champions of our time back then and won the Rugby league competition. It was no small wonder as half the team were Aboriginal kids and they were the speedy back-line whilst us white kids played the slow line in the forwards. My job was to get to the ball quickly, win the ball in scrums and be there as second assist in the tackles. Gary on the other hand was a back and carried the ball at great speed and tackled like a demon when we were in defence. Apart from our school association I sometimes caught up with him on weekends when we went to collect birds eggs for our hobby and often ventured into the bush to kill birds, lizards and snakes as a pastime. Something I am not so proud of, for now I have to think twice before I swat a fly or kill a cockroach.

Garry was well educated, having been a lawyer for many years before alcoholism got the better of him and he quit to go walkabout to beat his addiction. We had that as a common denominator, although we both arrived at our sober destination by different routes. As the sun set in the West the children emerged to sit at Elder Gary's feet, for he did not just teach them song line stories of which he was well versed in the old language, but he also taught the coastal language of his ancestors.It was in the telling that he commenced to the song line of the old Emu.

Apparently the Emu creator spirit flew across our vast continent to look over all the land. Now that the stars were apparent in the night sky, Gary The Elder turned there and pointed to the space between the stars of the Southern Cross. "If you look closely he said, you will see in the cloud between the most northern star is the Emu's head and to the middle lay its body and legs where it runs toward the milky way." He continued: "See, it tells us now when and where to collect the Emu eggs." To prove his song line story he produced two large Emu eggs from his carry sack to add credence to his tale. ary the elder then pointed to the constellation of the stars down as the belt of the Orion. As he told the song-line story of three boys who went out fishing in a canoe, but all they could find was the sacred Kingfish. The boy, not finding any other fish, was very hungry, so they caught and ate the Kingfish. The Sun God was very angry with them and created a water sprout which blew them in their canoe into the sky as a warning to other boys to obey tribal law. "So as you look toward Orion you can see on either end the front and the back of the canoe. You can see also from the thinner circle of Orion, the three boys trapped there and from the nebula where the new stars are born, for there lay the kingfisher."

Gary, as a rather young elder, recalling the first of what we know as 'baby boomers,' was appointed as a fully fledged teacher of the old ways of the tribesman. He told the dreamtime stories with some embellishment for the consumption of his young student; the Sun God Creator in his next story : "The Sun God gets on living in the morning and the red Ochre we see during the daylight hours. She brings us to her duty. She is a lovely old lady who fires up a stringy bark branch and carries it across the sky to give us light and heat. When it rains the bush is extinguished leaving the sky grey and it remains so until the rains cease, whereupon the old daily Sun relights the stringy bark and continues to bring light and the red glow across the sky, and the red earth of the land." Then he added : "during the night she travels behind the earth and camps until daybreak to start her work all over again." As for the moon he tells another story: "The moon is a lazy old man called Ngalindi. He is big and fat and mostly round and he is lazy. His wives and children get angry with him because he does nothing. They chop him up into smaller bits until they get thinner and thinner. They turn him into quarters each month with only one slice to appear in the sky, slowly returning quarter by quarter until he is a full Moon again. He never seems to learn his lesson of being useful and so the wives and children cut him up again and eventually he dies and come back to life after three days.

He cursed his wives and children and told them that he could continue to come back to life on each full Moon, but warned that other moons and stars would not return but remain dead. It is hope that at some stage he will be a useful moon of nature someday.`` The rainbow serpent was the next tale, Gary then told: "There was once a story of ghost riders known as Waglag. The legends tell the story when the sisters were traveling together, the older sister gave birth and her blood flowed to a waterhole where the rainbow serpent lives. It was also told by the ancient elders that the rainbow serpent was angered by the presence of the sisters in his area. Upon awakening and smelling the blood traces the scent to the elder sister sleeping in a hut, a metaphor for the womb of the sister. The rainbow serpent enters the hut and eats both sisters and their offspring. However, the rainbow serpent regurgitates them after being bitten by an ant, and the act creates Arnhem land. Now the rainbow serpent, in the form of an elder, speaks in their voices and teaches sacred rituals to the people living there."

 The Star dream story was a favourite of the old elders and Gary got delight in the telling of it: "The Star dream covers more than half the continent, from the deep centre of the desert through all the tribes' language groups. The story tells of seven sisters who make up the cluster of stars known as the Pleiades, in the constellation of Taurus." The story also appeared in ancient Greek mythology, Elder Gary, observing from Central Australia points out to the children at his feet how these small clusters of stars appear to keep a low trajectory above the horizon just after the sunset, giving the impression that they come from the earth and not the sky. In the Seven sister story, the group of stars are the Napaljarri sisters and also the vicinity is Jakamarra, a man of Wardilyka, who is in love with one of the women.

So the Elder told of how the Jakamarra man paints the morning star which still shines in the sky and he tells it as his 'Jukurra Jukurra' story. "He is the Jakamurra man who is in love with all the seven sisters of Napaljarri and can be seen chasing them across the night sky. They are seen to be running away from the man who wants to take one of the sisters for his wives, but under the traditional law, he is of the wrong skin group and is forbidden to take any of the sisters for a wife." As we look across the desert, the sisters appear in the shadows running away from the man as they travel across the land and before our very eyes they launch themselves from a hilltop in the shadows of the moonlight into the sky in the attempt to escape.

 Gary the Elder continued: "The Jampijinpa man follows the sisters in the form of a star seen in the Orion belt star cluster which can also be seen at the base of the Big Dipper. So every night the skin group of the seven sisters launch themselves skyward and become stars, closely followed by the Jampijinpa man who follows them across the sky. These storylines closely follow the skin group traditions of the home tribes of one skin group and that of the man and are deeply connected with tribal law and the sacred men's group ceremonies too." Gary the elder tells the children of the Star dreaming stories of the different tribes. The journeys of the Japaljarri men who travel the North near Kurlungali Pa in the lajapamanu meaning to the North, the law and the initiations ceremonies. So it was that Gary the Elder ceased his dreamtime telling once more. He hinted of time-in stories to come,-of the crocodile who cleared the land with his tail and forced the ocean to run to the central continent. The desert sun dried up the land for where the crocodile is reported to live to this day. He also told of the importance of the fire, wind and the rain and he promised to tell more in our next meeting. However, there was one more song- line story he wished to tell that evening for it related to both our Christian upbringing and that of his Aboriginal ancestors. He had somehow combined the Christian story of Christmas, the Virgin Mary and that of the child Jesus with that of the Aboriginal dreamtime. I felt this story was as much for my belief as that of the children as we sat now by the fire, for it was the twilight hour and the evening was getting chilly.

So my once childhood friend, now an Aboriginal elder, began to tell the story: "It was a night like no other, a night of nature and human miracles. For it took place some two thousand years ago on the other side of the world. For the first miracle was that there were no stars in the heavens anywhere, save for one diamond brilliant star that moved across the silken twilight sky-scape from the west down to the east. It settled over a little village outside the city of Jerusalem, over a barn on the edge of the city and has remained in that position in the sky ever since. We have been drawn to call it the Evening Star. Shepherds tending their sheep on a far off hill were drawn to the sight, as they had previously dreamed of this night in a vision and now it was reality. On a far away plain to the West were three wise Kings on camels who had been following the star trajectory. They too had dreamed of this night and came with symbolic gifts of gold for kingship, that of frankincense as symbol of a deity, and myrrh, and embracing oils as symbol of death; not of imminent death but that of a sign of mortality." The storyteller of magic dream time stopped for a moment, took a deep breath and continued his dream time story.

"The shepherds likewise came with a gift of a baby lamb, which became symbolic, for it represented the lamb of God." Gary the Elder turned his attention then to the night sky and pointed out the sign of Virgo, the Virgin queen. On her head were the stars representative of the Mother of the chosen one and at her feet it appeared a snake being crushed by her feet, representative of Christ's power over evil. Then beneath her feet also were twelve stars all of which ultimately represented the twelve Apostles. The miracle of the dream had Mary the mother being visited by the Archangel Gabriel as commanded by God. He told her that she would have a son and he would be the greatest of living beings and would perform great miracles and teach the word of God. At the same time her betrothed, Joseph the carpenter also had a dream in which the angel came and told him that his son would be a King, but not of this world and that he was to be baptized as Yeshua, which in Hebrew is 'to deliver, to rescue.' So it was that Joseph married Mary and she was filled with the spirit of the Lord. Joseph then selected the strongest of his young donkeys which he called 'the carrier.' For it was the duty of this beast of burden to carry the Mother with the child on his back all the way to Jerusalem. Romans insisted that all peoples throughout the land join in the Census for historic record and the payment of future taxes. Upon arrival in the city of Jerusalem and finding no accommodation due to the crowds for the census, they settled in an animal manger at the rear of an inn on the outskirts of the city.

 Gary the Elder sat with me by the dying embers of the fire as we recalled our childhood years and the teaching of the Nuns. "Those teachers had us believe that the mother held the child to her breast as she carried him, but we Aboriginals, we see it differently." He pointed once more to the star sign of Virgo and stated. "It was under this sign that the child was born. Its when Leo crossed over Virgo there see…and Jupiter came out nine months later." He then went on to describe the pattern within the stars and I visualized what he was looking at. There I visualized what my black brother saw as the Madonna. The features of the face were intriguing; she had a noticeable air of self possession about her. Madonna's face was clearly delineated much like what one sees in Renaissance art work of her, but clearly a living individual. Instead of carrying her son on her lap, he sat upon her shoulder and she held one ankle with her left hand and the right across his hip to ensure he did not lose balance. She was fashionable in the style of the Aboriginal women of the Tiwi islands and Daly river country and she walked with style and pride of achievement.

  I came out of that vision and my friend with a big toothy smile and penetrating black eye that shone in the darkness said: " Now you get it right?"

I could not deny what I saw but was keen to discuss further the thoughts and feelings this Aboriginal of my childhood had interpreted as a Christian faith. There seem to be some dreamtime song lines written into their interpretations. As a doubting Thomas so to speak, in my wandering through life, I had finally settled on a manifested Jesus as my Higher power in whom I could trust to guide and protect me. It had been until now the only way I could see my way clearly to maintain some belief in God. Still I continued to enquire and be interested in the viewpoint of my Aboriginal brother. I asked: "Gary, remember we were taught of the Trinity of God the Father, Son and Holy Ghost, three persons in the one God, how do you see that as an indigenous man ? Do you think that the Christ we were taught about was of a divine nature? Was he really a Deity?" Gary suddenly turned back to the scriptures in his mind and the matter of the teachings. I remembered that he was once a well respected lawyer before the booze caught up with him, as it had done with me. He had walked the desert of Arnhem land to soothe the savage beast within and I had walked the Camino de Santiago in my letting go of pain and the grip of the grape.

Gary thought for some time before giving his answer on the deity of Jesus of Nazareth and answered:" We were taught by those Irish Nuns on the point of the Trinity if you may recall." He then continued: " Those Nuns had the logical linear means to explain it all, but they used their imagination to get us all in touch with the Spirit right? I did not reply, having struggled with this for much of my adult life and preferred to wait for him to continue: " I am like you in this belief Doug, but am also guided by my family and ancestors too. I believe that the Infinite Intelligence which we choose to call God, breathes his spirit into Christ at his birth. He had already ordained that he was to be the one who was destined to be called deity, but he had to earn his stripes so to speak. So, in the biblical sense, this child of the heavenly realm came to earth just like any other human. He was given the free will and task to offer himself in the service of the Father in heaven. So he was not divine whilst on earth but had a spiritual link beyond the people of his time. The method he chose by his suffering and death on the cross, possibly shocked even God his Master in heaven. The reward of course was that he opened up the channel for us to link with the Holy Ghost, or Holy Spirit as he is more commonly known now. It was not until he suffered and died and ascended into the heavenly realm that he took on the role of a Deity, but as we assume without full proof, he did walk this earth, but not as a Deity but as man."

I was quite taken by what Gary the elder had to say, and I had to admit to myself that it left me in no doubt but to turn to meditation, to take another look at the journey of Christ from that Christmas birth until the day of his death on the cross, and his ascension into the heavens. So I left my friend Gary the elder, promising that I would return to hear more of his dreamtime stories and set about once more to find a place to meditate, think over my non-belief and somehow ask for guidance in that part of me, of my imagination in the belief of a manifested Christ. I returned to my place of abode with the mission of rising early the next morning to meditate a little further on my own belief and of a way to tell here the story like the Aborigines of old told their song-lines. In truth, before hearing Gary the elder's teaching of a mixture of Aboriginal story-line and of the Christianity we both had been conditioned to; I had heard the Aboriginal story-line of the birth of a certain God who had a black son who emerged from a black star in the sky. The star had died and left a spirit star to rule and guide the tribes. It was the same star we call the Evening Star, the brightest star forever in our Eastern Australian sky.

From the stillness of the night sky I heard the voice of the hunter calling: When I am hunting in the bush, among the trees, on a hill or beside a billabong; I am in the presence of God. It is in our natural environment that we feel close to the Creator. We do not hurry him, we let nature take its course whatever the weather or season, event or ceremony. We watch the man on the moon as he is reflected to us. We wait for God and nature to fill the rivers and water the thirsty earth as much as we accept the dry landscape in another season. At twilight we are preparing for the night's hunt. At dawn we rise with the sun. We watch the bush food ripen before we gather, wait for our young to grow though their initiation ceremonies. We take time in sorrow to mourn our deceased and allow plenty of time for grieving. We abide our time for meetings and ceremonies ensuring that the right people are present before we commit. We do not mind waiting because we want things to be done right. There is no hurry, we are all in God's time which is the right time. We await him to make up his mind and be guided by the answers that are always forthcoming if we care to listen."

There is much documented evidence, in the Bible and other credible recorded literature that confirms the reality of a Christ on earth story. I had come to believe after much outward and inward mourning that one either has belief in Christ or a disbelief. My subconscious mind, through all my trials and tribulations of my life journey, still wavered between the real and the unreal of the mythology of a living Christ. It was perhaps easier to just accept that there was a Christ who walked this earth, taught great truths, performed miracles, was crucified, died then rose again and ascended body and soul into the heavenly realm. It was no longer my concern. The dreamtime of the Aboriginal song line stories of Christ-God, birth, death and his rising from the dead in the dreamtime; Christ of the Christian symbolism, Christ of the Roman times, of Biblical proportion, of association with the Father-God of infinite intelligence. The stories told as myth or as real were a matter now of my subconscious mind unfolding. For I had come to believe in a power greater than self through much suffering. Like so many others, a doubting Thomas of pacified disbelief, Jesus' earthly existence came as with that of the risen Christ. Be it a mythical story or reality, it meant that he had risen to my way of thinking. It was not of the rational, linear conscious belief that I had now turned and turned into, but to the manifested belief in a risen Christ, a Christ in the manifest was my belief now. It was Christ I turned to in a spirit of harmony, forgiveness and guidance.

So it was that I made my way, in the dawning light of the morning sun, after the night of mythical discovery with Gary the elder. I, in my own way, now had the need to focus on meditation into my own dream time as it were. To find in my own scaffolding of my logical brain on the other side of the imagination, an imitation of Christ's discovery and tells the story like an Aboriginal dreamtime tale, if not only for my own spiritual satisfaction, but for those of you who read this little book.

We, the people of this earth, black, white, red and yellow on a white background are coloured in the clouds of the rainbow spirit, of the spirit of the bright moon, of the blazing sun, of the red earth, of the dark earth, the rivers, the waters, the plants and the animals, and of the dreamtime, the descendants of song-lines and painted images on cave walls. We are the present-day images of the Gods we believe in collectively and individually, of one true creator, of the manifestation of a Son, a holy Higher Self or spirit linked to the Creator God, the Father of all Fathers, the ghost who exists as a pale reflection of ourselves as we gaze into small ponds.

We are the Aboriginal man who goes walkabout in the deserts, in dreamtime with the Creator. We are the red man who sits in a tepee tent smoking a peace pipe, in touch with his ancestors in the black hills of Dakota, negro man of Africa offering a sacrificial prayer to his God, Jewish man with a sacrificial lamb, the white man of sacrificial Christ, the Buddhists who meditate into their spirituality, the adherents of Islam who believe in Mohammed of the desert. Such are this world's manifestations that are meant to bring peace not war, to encourage wise men to make amends for wrongdoing, to progress forward into the light and not return to the darkness; these are the myths, legends and folklore that will make this generation and future generations all the better for continuing our respective beliefs.

So with all my digging into Canon Law, myths, symbolism and signs in the sky, I had to admit that I had now recognised that my dignity and that of God's own nature was the pathway of Christianity. That God does not want me, nor any man to return to our former nature where defects of character were the basis for living. For in embracing the Mass, the reenactment of the act of receiving Christ body and blood in the Eucharist we are brought out of the power of darkness into the light of the Kingdom of God. It was through thoughts of the the Aboriginal legends, the myths surrounding miracles of the past and the reality of some, biblical stories of the coming of our saviour, and the New Testament teaching of Matthew, Mark, Luke and John and the evangelism of Paul's teaching of Christ that I realized "the symbol of faith" confesses the greatness of God's gift to man in his work of creation. And even more so in his redemption and sanctification. The faith that confessed that we are all children of God through Christ's communion sacrament of rebirth, in our partaking of his divine nature. I was coming to an adult reasoning that we are all called to henceforth lead a life worthy of the gospel of Christ. That we are all capable of doing this by the grace of Christ, by the gift of the Spirit, which we receive through the sacraments and prayer.

Not that I had not reasoned this through the steps of AA. Firstly in Step 2, coming to realize that there is a power greater than self. And then in Step 3, handing over to that power, and Step 11, "Sought through prayer and meditation to improve our conscious contact with God as we understood Him, praying only for knowledge of His will for us and the power to carry that out" and then Step 12; "Having had a spiritual awakening as the result of these steps, we tried to carry this message to alcoholics, and to practice these principles in all affairs."

And yet, whilst it quells the desire for the Step conscious sober alcoholic to consider those still suffering alcoholics who have not as yet handed over to a God of their own understanding, it does not entirely fulfil the spiritual thirst, whereas the partaking of the Eucharist within a Christian religious faith does. It now seems apparent to me that I need both. One that answers my logical linear mind set of belief and another that fulfils my manifested belief of handing over to a creator Christ to remain sober, with a Trinity in the God centre, which fulfils the promise of salvation.

CHAPTER 10.

THE LIFE IN CHRIST

It seems that the spirit of grace, through the third person of the Trinity enters one's soul at that time. Salvation grace for smooth sailing on the waters of life. How is it so that some Catholics can under Canon Law do this, whilst others can not? Is it because we are freed from sin by God in his Trinity of salvation, or does it still mean that a renegade like me in mortal sin (a grievous state against the law of God) should abstain from receiving such grace by partaking of the Communion because I have not been justifiably absolved from my sin by receiving absolution from a priest in personal confession? I repeat, as I have done elsewhere in this book, the priest in the Mass celebration, before administering communion to the congregation prayers: "Take this, all of you, and drink from it, for this is the chalice of my blood, the blood of the new and eternal covenant which will be poured out for you and for many for the forgiveness of sins. Do this in memory of me."

At the very beginning of Mass, Catholics make a type of confession of sins, declaring their faults before the whole congregation. Afterward, the priest recites a formula that appears to absolve their sins at Mass. The priest typically says the following words. *May almighty God have mercy on us, forgive us our sins and bring us to everlasting life.* What can be confusing is that sometimes particular priests or the people in the pews will make the sign of the cross, as if they were in the confessional. While the opening rites of Mass may mimic some of the acts of confession, in reality this is far from any type of "general confession" or "general absolution." The General instruction of the Roman Missal clearly states this distinction. *After this, the Priest calls upon the whole community to take part in the Penitential Act, which, after a brief pause for silence, it does by means of a formula of general confession. The rite concludes with the Priest's absolution, which, however, lacks the efficacy of the Sacrament of Penance. It is also generally accepted that the congregation make a sign of the cross in acknowledgment of the forgiveness of minor (venial) sin and major (mortal) sin.*

So it is now up to me to determine if I adhere to what was incorporated into Christ by my baptism that I be " dead to sin and alive to God in Christ Jesus" and so participate in the life of the Risen Lord. (Romans 6:11) To strive to be as taught an "imitator" of God as a beloved child, and walk in love, like in the Epiphany 5:1-2. It seems that to achieve a sacred status by thought, word and deed, to be the mind in Christ Jesus we must follow his example (John 13:12). To be justified in the name of Jesus and the Spirit of God (1 Cor 6:11) sanctified and called to be saints (1 Cor 1:2), to be Christian is the need to become the temple of the Holy Spirit (1 Cor.6:19) and having become the 'Trinity life' we must act as to bear "the fruit of the Spirit." (Gal 5:22,25) by charity in action. We must heal the wounds of our defects of character and be renewed by the Holy Spirit in a Spiritual transformation.(Eph. 4:23). We are called to be "children of the light" through "all that is good and right and true." (Eph 5:8,9.) What an order, how can I do that?

In a discussion with a Christian friend over coffee who is not of the Catholic faith, he summed it up like this: " We must purge ourselves of our wrongdoing." I took this as confession and absolution from God with the view to sin no more. "Then there is the need to uncover the barrier to progress in our unconscious mind." This may take a lot of work with one's confessor, spiritual guide or in some cases a psychologist. For it will undoubtedly bring up barriers to progress that must be cleared before one is free to move forward.

Then, as my friend said,: "There is the final stage, the union with God." This one is often misread by those of warm and fuzzy feeling faith who advocate a 'justifiable' acceptance that we are all humans of perfect and imperfect nature, and as such it's acceptable to God to excuse ourselves. It's kind of a cop out but a good start if you will. St. Paul insists that the law is holy and good in the sense that it reveals to all who try to follow it just how very sinful we are. The law shows us that no matter how good our intentions, we still end up in sin and in need of the deliverance available only through faith in Jesus. "I do not understand what I do. For what I want to do I do not do, but what I hate I do. ... And if I do what I do not want to do, I agree that the law is good. (Romans 7:15-20). This passage gives us the first-hand account of the battle between the new nature and the sinful flesh within the apostle Paul. He writes these verses as a mature believer in Christ. Paul's own life demonstrates that this struggle with sinful flesh never goes away while we are on the earth. Paul further explains it in Romans 7: "Thanks be to God, who delivers me through Jesus Christ our Lord! So then, I myself in my mind am a slave to God's law, but in my sinful nature a slave to my flesh." Then in Romans 8:9, "You, however, are not in the flesh but in the Spirit, if in fact the Spirit of God dwells in you. Anyone who does not have the Spirit of Christ does not belong to him. But ye are not in the flesh, but in the Spirit, if so be that the Spirit of God dwells in you."

So the way of Christ leads to life, whilst a contrary way leads to destruction. (Matthew 7:13) The gospel parable of the two ways remains ever present in the education of believers to the Canon Law of the Church, for it shows the importance of moral decisions for our salvation of which one way leads to life eternal whilst the other leads to death, for there is a great difference in the two. So am I to follow the dictates of the Church or soldier on with my own acceptance of Christ, the forgiveness of my defects, be they 'venial' or 'mortal' in nature. Perhaps the last words should always be in Christ himself, who reportedly said: " I am the way, the truth and the life: no man comes to the Father, but by me. I am. I am the door: by me if any man enters, he ..."John 10:9.

I ask you to consider that our Lord Jesus Christ is your true head, and that you are one of his members. He belongs to you as the head belongs to its members; all that is his is yours: his spirit, his heart, his body and soul, and all his faculties. You must make use of all these as of your own, to serve, praise, love, and glorify God. You belong to him, as members belong to their head. And so he longs for you to use all that is in you, as if it were his own, for the service and glory of the Father. [25] For me, to live is Christ. The divine image is present in every man. It shines forth as the communion of persons, in the likeness of the union of divine persons among themselves. Endowed with " a spiritual and immortal " soul the human person is '" the only creature on earth that God has willed for his own sake." (Genesis 24.) From his conception, he is destined for eternal beatitude. The human person participates in the light and power of the divine Spirit. By his reason, he is capable of understanding the order of things established by the Creator. By his free will, he is capable of directing himself toward his true good. He finds his perfection "in seeking and loving what is true and good. By virtue of his soul and his spiritual powers of intellect and will, man is endowed with freedom, an outstanding manifestation of the divine image. By his reason, man recognises the voice of God which urges him to do what is good and avoid what is evil." (Genesis 16.) it is not just Biblical law it is Canon Law too. It's the Catechism of the Catholic Church.

Everyone is obliged to follow this law, which makes itself heard in conscience and is fulfilled in the love of God and neighbour. Living a moral life bears witness to the dignity of the person. "Man enticed by the Evil One, abused his freedom at the beginning of history." (Genesis 13.) He succumbed to temptation and did what was evil. He still desires the good, but his nature bears the wound of original sin. He is now inclined to evil and subject to error. Man is divided in himself. As a result, the whole of men, both individual and social, shows itself to be a struggle, and a dramatic one, between good and evil, between light and darkness. But his Passion, Christ delivered us from Satan and from sin. He merited us with a new life in the Holy Spirit. His grace restores what sin had damaged in us. (The Catechism of the Catholic Church).

A picture of Mary the mother of Jesus came to mind when I drifted back to the French route of the Camino in the spring of 2017. Walking with Ian, the English solicitor, having left Santo Domingo early in the cool of the morning, we had made good time on our destination to Belorado an ancient Roman township some 23 km away. There were no great hills to climb and frequent small villages offered some respite and services for breaks on the journey. We had stopped at the village of Redecilla del Camino, 11 km from our starting point that day. Seated at a pavement cafe drinking coffee, we began a conversation about the Immaculate Conception of Mary. Ian was born into the Church of England and my own Catholic upbringing made for an interesting discussion with mutual agreed respect for the Mother of Jesus. We both had accepted the doctrine taught by our faiths that neither of us practiced anymore. The main difference was his mistaken belief Catholics pray to Mary for spiritual and material needs instead of the Anglican belief that one prayed directly to Christ. I pointed out that Catholics did not pray 'to' Mary but 'through' her to intercede on believers' behalf. I had stopped at a small Church just before my farewell to Ian, recalling our past conversation on Mary's Conception and by a strange coincidence, the Church was called the Immaculate Conception. It was closed for afternoon siesta, so I took a card on offer with a picture of Our Lady of Fatima statue on the front from the brochure box at the Church door and read the prayer on the back. "Fatima Prayer of Reparation. Father, Son and Holy Spirit I adore thee profoundly. I offer the Body, Blood, Soul and Divinity of Jesus Christ; in reparation for the outrages, sacrileges and indifferences by which he is offended."

A few kilometers along the Way I sat and stared at that prayer card and a piece of paper caught my attention so I picked it up to read it. It was a shiny card which held an element of surprise for me. One side was a picture of the Virgin Mary as she may have appeared to the children of Fatima with radiant light pouring from her hands. It was a carbon copy of a bronze Medallion similar to the one I had as a teenager when I belonged to the Holy Name Society. The Fatima connection with card signs and medallion symbolism sat well with the Catholic teachings of my youth. Whilst I did not practice the faith anymore, I never-the-less missed the rituals and the symbolism that the universal philosophy of faith provided me. I had been given a gold embossed medallion of Christ image taken from the shroud of Turin when on the Camino in 2013. I recalled a natural symbol of a golden sun, the nature of God and the letters IHS. The Sisters of Mercy taught us as children that it stood for 'I have suffered.' In fact, it is a monogram for the name 'Jesus Christ' in Latin but initially came from the Greek letters chi (X) and rho (P). The Chi-Rho symbol is often portrayed with an (A) Alpha on one side of the X and (O) Omega on the other side; Jesus Christ, the beginning and the end. This symbol most remembered by Jews and Christians alike, traditionally was different, the letters INRI were engraved then nailed on a plague, above the head of the dead Christ on the Cross. It was written in three languages; Hebrew, Greek and Latin. In English, it has a similar meaning: 'Jesus the Nazarene, King of the Jews.' Reportedly, the Jewish Priest at the time of the crucifixion asked Pilate, the Roman Governor, who condemned Christ to death at the bequest of the Jewish mob, to change the plague to read "He called himself the King of the Jews." Pilate's response was. "What I have written, I have written." On the track I found another medallion and on the front it had a symbol of the rays of the sun. I thought that it could equally have been the Camino symbol: the Scallop shell depicting all roads leading to Santiago, the Way of St. James that ultimately leads to the mystery and myth in and around the Santiago Cathedral.

My mind once more on myths and secrets took me back to that morning in Santarem, Portugal. I had searched the town enquiring about the Fatima legend. The funny little proprietor in my private hotel did not know where Fatima was. I thought it strange knowing from my guide book that it was not far by road from Santarem, but not realizing at the time that I should have been asking for the Way to Coimbra. I thought of the mystery of Rosary beads that linked to Fatima given to me by the two young Canadian female teachers on my first Camino and the list of the decades of the Rosary they had written down for me.

Maybe the Mysteries of the Rosary was the key to what the Fatima apparitions were all about? Mary, the Mother of Jesus, had called herself 'Our Lady of The Rosary' in those apparitions. I had lost the Rosary beads in 'Refugio' on my first Camino and justified that loss by the presumption that some other Pilgrim would find more meaning from meditating on the repetitive mantra and the meanings of each bead of the decades than this Pilgrim who had not even bothered to pray on them at all. At last a bus from Santarem to Fatima arrived and the journey was around two hours which gave me ample time to consider the reasons for my visit, specifically to go to the place where Mary, Our Lady, the Mother of Jesus, reportedly appeared to three little shepherd kids in 1917. I was skeptical of the reality of the apparitions that the children of Fatima had reportedly experienced, but I was keen to explore the myth, the fantasy and the facts. A great flow of pilgrims to the site had been constant for the past 100 years and many books, films and songs had been written on the subject: The 'Miracle of Fatima' and the life and death of those 'saintly' little ones.

I began to put pen to paper, intent to recreate a biographical sketch of the lives of the three little shepherds and the mysterious appearance of Mary, Mother of Jesus, the Son of God, to a remote field near the little village of Fatima. "On the 30th day of March, 1907, a female child was baptized of the name Lucia, born at Aljustrel on the 22nd day of March of the same year, at 7 o'clock in the evening.' So said the Parish Register a copy of which I was later privileged to be furnished with a copy. As the youngest of seven children, six girls and one boy, Lucia was the family favorite and surrounded with affection from her earliest childhood. Family circumstances obliged Lucia to start out life at an early age as a shepherdess. Her initial companions were the girls and boys of Aljustrel and its surroundings. From 1917, her young cousins, Jacinta and Francisco Marto, were her sole companions. That was the year in which Mary appeared to them. Lucia had a special role during the vision spoken only to her and gave her the message which was only to be revealed at a future date.

She lived and suffered, together with her cousins, on account of the apparitions. She alone remained on earth for a longer period in order to fulfill her mission. She started attending school only after the apparitions but, with her talents and her good memory, she learned to read and write very quickly. As soon as the apparitions were over, Lucia found herself in the position of a 'seer', with all the dangers resulting therefrom. Something, therefore, had to be done about her. One of the primary interests of the new Bishop of the re-established Dioceses of Leiria was her education. The Bishop tried to quarantine her from the dangers threatening her in the pervasive atmosphere of the time. On the morning of June 17th 1921, she entered the College of the Sisters of St. Dorothy at Vilar which is now a suburb of Porto.

The first secret, apart from the recommendation by Mary of penance, sacrifice and prayer, was her prediction that Lucia's two cousins Francisco and Juanita would die soon, which they did within three years of what became known as the miracles of Fatima. The second secret appeared to predict the end of the First World War, the Bolshevik revolution and its effect on Christian faith and the start of the Second World War. Lucia quoted the Virgin Mary as saying: "Russia will spread its errors around the world, promoting wars and persecutions of the church. She said later that, being a child, she assumed at the time that 'Russia' was 'a women, a bad women." The third prophecy had the Virgin Mary speaking of a 'bishop dressed in white', who would 'fall to the ground as though dead under gunfire.' It was kept secret by the Vatican throughout the 20th Century, officials being fearful that it might encourage an attack on Church leaders, including the Pope. Only in 2000 did the Vatican reveal this third prophecy- rather conveniently, according to lesser believers- suggesting that it referred to the assassination attempt on Pope John Paul 11 by Mehmet Ali Agca in St. Peters Square in 1981.

The date of the attempt, May 13th, the same as that which the little shepherds had first seen their apparition back in 1917 added credibility to the theory, and the Pope subsequently visited the shrine at Fatima to give thanks for his survival. He took with him one of the gunman's 9mm bullets, which he placed in the crown of the Virgin statue. The Pope often made it clear that he believed Lucia's visions had saved his life. It seems likely that she too will be beatified after the appropriate passing of years. The fear of Russia being the catalyst to a future Armageddon was lessoned after the end of World War 11 where much of the predictions of Fatima had come to pass. It appears that the Catholic Church, despite unknowns surrounding secrets, still appears to relegate the third secret to a thing of the past. Pope John Paul 11 in union with the Bishops consecrated Russia to the Immaculate Heart of Mary on March 25th, 1984. In addition to the consecration of Russia, Pope Pius X11, Pope Benedict XV1 and Pope Francis also consecrated the world to the Immaculate heart.

How could little children in a rural town in Portugal predict the rise and fall of Russia in the Twentieth Century? What of the sun dancing in the sky at the last apparition in 1917? This was a spectacular event witnessed by a crowd of 70,000 people. Was the unusual phenomenon of January 25th 1938 when the world at large saw dancing lights in the sky in the same class as the dancing of the sun of October 13th 1917? Was this a prediction of the Second World War being imminent? Our Lady had predicted '"The war is going to end (World War1) But if men do not cease offending God...another worse one will begin in the reign of Pius X1 ...Russia will spread its errors throughout the world, causing wars and the persecutions against the Church. When you see a night illumed by an unknown light, know that it is the great sign given you by God that he is about to punish the world for its crimes, by means of war, famine and persecutions against the Church and the Holy Father..." Was the third secret related to the assassination attempt on Pope John Paul 11 or the tragic death of Pope John Paul the first on September 29th 1978?

Our Lady of Fatima is the approved apparition of Mary in the 20th century, a time which witnessed a number of reported appearances of the Virgin. Are we entering the end times that are prophesied by the Book of Revelation? While private revelation, such as apparitions, are a matter of faith, one cannot ignore the healing miracles and profound effect of historical apparitions like the existence of Christ on this earth- his revelation, his teachings, his death and resurrection. One can choose to ignore or believe as a matter of faith, like Fatima: the reality of his being or the spiritual essence of a living Christ within the manifest. The Catholic Church has approved other apparitions of Mary since the first in 40 AD. According to legend, in January of that year, the Apostle James the Greater was meditating on the shores of the Ebor River in Spain. The conversion of souls to Christ was not going well for James as the occult was as strong in the Galicia province as it is today. Mary miraculously appeared in the flesh on a pillar of stone carried by Angels, calling for his return to Jerusalem. The Pillar is supposed to be the same one Christ lent upon when he was scourged under the instruction of Pilot, the Roman Governor.

The New Testament states that, when Christ died, was buried and rose again from the dead after three days, he appeared to his disciples. Thomas was absent from the room the first time. When told of Christ's appearance, he stated: 'Unless I touch the wounds of his hands and the side that was pierced, I shall not believe. (John 20:25) Jesus returned once more to the disciples and asked Thomas to touch the wounds of his hands and the side that was pierced. When Thomas had done as instructed, he bowed down before Christ saying 'My lord and my God. Jesus replied "Blessed are you Thomas because you have seen and believe. Blessed are they also that have not seen yet still believe." (John 20:29) My skeptical mind, like Thomas, still doubted the mystery and the miracles of Fatima. However, the myths, legend and folklore of the events of Fatima were outweighed by the documented letters of Lucia, the dancing sun newspaper article and the verification of the masses of witnesses; the photo of Juanita's body on the opening of her coffin in 1935, these I had sighted at Fatima and my mind and spirit was leaning towards acceptance. It was Sunday morning and the Mass outside the little chapel at Fatima, in the now concrete field of Cova da Iria was well underway when I arrived there. The masses of men, women and children stood singing in unison during this High Mass. The Bishops and priest's solemn services could hardly be heard from the distant altar at the base of the hilly slope below.

Many people crawled on their knees on the concrete pathway toward the celebration of Communion for the faithful. The audio equipment amplified the priests mantra as he served the host "Body of Christ " he repeated. He spoke in Portuguese, but I could hear the message in English in my head. Pushing my way through the crowd to the actual location of the miracles where a statue built in 1921 stands. I looked up at the crown on the statue. A replica of The Lady of the Rosary, where the 9mm caliber assassin's bullet, left there by Pope John Paul 11m rests in peace. The crowd was closing in and many believers, both young and old, were crawling around and around the foot of the statue. I recited a quick prayer and left; I never did like crowds except at a rock concert. Making my way to the rear of the church to a small enclosure, I found I was in the crypt where the three little children of Fatima now lay. An Irishman, presumably a priest in sheep's clothing, was kneeling with a very attractive middle aged nun like Irish women at the foot of Francisco and Juanita's final burial site. But perhaps they were lovers or maybe just lay pilgrims and not clergy at all? Both were reciting the last sorrowful mystery of the Rosary and I felt compelled to pray.

We chatted briefly beside the burial site of Lucia in that crypt, her final resting place, a little distance from her two young cousins who are buried side by side. I explained my purpose in coming to Fatima on my second Camino. They both wished me well with a blessing as the Irish do and I left for a further look around Fatima. None the wiser for my experience at that time, I checked out the library, the book store and writings of Lucia within the church grounds for clues to my verification of the apparitions. Making my way to the streets, there was a smorgasbord of memorabilia for sale on Miracles of Fatima, statues of Mary, Rosary beads by the hundreds, books one could not climb over, hand crafts, copies of 'authenticated' writings of Lucia, black and white photos of the children in a garden, Lucia and Jacinta and Francisco, footnoted 'September 1917'. This was where the Angel reportedly once appeared, as represented in the third apparition of the Angel. The Monument stood close by to the crypt, the burial ground of the three shepherd children. I had enough of monuments and the commercial traders in the streets of Fatima, so I settled for a sidewalk cafe to watch the passing parade and ate lunch and stayed sipping on a strong Portuguese coffee, perhaps the most enjoyable part of my Fatima visit. I felt sure the commercialisation of Our Lady of the Fatima was not the intended result hoped for by Mary or the children of Fatima, but it was sure bringing in the Euros.

As I travelled on the bus back to Santarem I got to contemplating the words of now deceased Pope Benedict XV1 on his 2010 visit to Fatima as he addressed 500,000 pilgrims and the millions that watched on TV affirming strongly: "The Fatima Prophecy is not accomplished. There will be more wars and more terrors." With the current ongoing wars in the Middle East, other hotbeds of unrest and terrorism rife throughout the western world, I had to agree. Where was Russia in this?

In logic and Mathematics, there is a method of inquiry called proof of contradiction, which establishes the truth of a proposition indirectly by demonstrating that the impossible for the proposition is false. In proof of this kind, we begin with two assertions, one being the negation of the other. Properly phrased, only one of the two statements 'can' be true, and one of them 'must' be true. In a classic example dating back to the ancient Greeks Euclid, which began with the following pair of opposite assertions: Either there are infinitely many prime numbers, or there are not infinitely many prime numbers. In the present time back then, as I rode that bus I began with a pair of statements: Either Our Lady of Fatima's request for the consecration of Russia has been satisfactorily heeded, or it has not been satisfactorily heeded.

Coming back to my assumptions, namely the Russia consecration as stated by Our Lady of Fatima in her third secret assertion leads to absurdity or to the contrary, that the assertion is known to be true. Assuming that the first statement of Our Lady of Fatima's request for the Consecration of Russia has been satisfactorily heeded and in the manner requested, a period of peace will be given to the world. Well, at no time since Our lady reportedly made that request, including the 30 plus years since Pope Paul 11 fulfilled the promised consecration of our world and consecrated Russia in that Fatima event in 1984, has there been peace throughout the world. And in no sense do we today have the security from the threat of a Nuclear Armageddon. The message of Fatima is still unfolding.

CHAPTER 11.

THE VISION OF BELIEF

Our Lady of Fatima is the approved apparition of Mary in the 20th century, a time which witnessed a number of reported appearances of the Virgin. Are we entering the end times that are prophesied by the Book of Revelation? While private revelation, such as apparitions, are a matter of faith, one cannot ignore the healing miracles and profound effect of historical apparitions like the existence of Christ on this earth- his revelation, his teachings, his death and resurrection. One can choose to ignore or believe as a matter of faith, like Fatima: the reality of his being or the spiritual essence of a living Christ within the manifest. The Catholic Church has approved other apparitions of Mary since the first in 40 AD. According to legend, in January of that year, the Apostle James the Greater was meditating on the shores of the Ebor River in Spain. The convert of souls to Christ was not going well for James, as the occult was as strong in the Galicia province as it is today. Mary miraculously appeared in the flesh on a pillar of stone carried by Angels, calling for his return to Jerusalem. The Pillar is supposed to be the same one Christ lent upon when he was scourged under the instruction of Pilot, the Roman Governor. Mary had requested St. James in that vision to build a church there in her honour. The building task resulted in a surge of conversions resulting in the growth of the Catholic faith in Spain. The chapel is one of the first chapels in all of Spain devoted to the Immaculate Conception This chapel like so many others throughout Christendom affirms that Jesus Christ has human nature in the sense that he was born of a human mother, the Virgin Mary. At the same time, despite being born of a human mother, Jesus also has divine nature because he was born of the Holy Spirit and not a human father. Jesus Christ is considered both man and God, fully divine and fully human. This is a doctrine of faith within Catholicism.

Man's vocation is to a life made up of divine charity and human solidarity. It is to be graciously offered up by following the way of Christ as a way to salvation. The dignity of the human person is rooted in his creation as in the image and likeness to our Creator. It is essential to a human being

So it is through the "image and likeness" to Christ, the Redeemer and Saviour that the divine image, disfigured by man by his wrongdoing, has been restored to its original beauty and ennobled by the grace of God. This divine image is present in every man. It shines forth in the communion of persons, in the likeness of the union of divine persons among themselves. For man is endowed with a " spiritual and immortal" soul. He is the only creature on earth that God has willed for his own sake. From his inception, he is destined for eternal grace and bliss. He participates in the light and power of the divine Spirit. By his reason, he is capable of understanding the order of things established by hisd Creator. By free will, he is capable of directing himself towards his true good. He finds his perfection " in seeking and loving what is true and good."(Genesis 15). By virtue of his soul and spiritual powers of intellect and will, man is endowed with freedom , an "outstanding manifestation of divine image" (Genesis 17)

By his reason, man recognises the voice of God which directs him to "do good and avoid evil." (Genesis 16) Everyone is obliged to follow this law, which in itself is heard in conscience and is fulfilled in the love of God and for his neighbours. Living a moral life bears witness to the dignity of the person. Man enticed by the Evil One, abused his freedom from the very beginning of history. Man has repeatedly succumbed to temptation and does what is evil. Man is divided in himself. As a result, the whole of men, both individual and social, shows itself as a struggle and a dramatic one, between what is good and what is evil, between what is light and what is darkness.

It is Catholic belief that by his passion, Christ delivered us from Satan and from sin which is inherent in our defects of character. He merits us the new life in the Holy Spirit. His grace restores what our wrongdoing had damaged in us. He who believes in Christ becomes a son of God. We are restored in our Creator by following the example of Christ. It makes us capable of acting rightly and doing good. In union with our Saviour we attain the perfection of charity which is holiness. Having matured in grace, the moral life begins to blossom into eternal life in the glory of heaven. God puts us in this world to know, to love and to serve him. The grace of God makes us partake of his divine nature, our participation in the Mass, by receiving the body and blood of Christ in the Eucharist. We therefore enter into the glory of God, and the joy of the Trinity with the grace bestowed upon us through the Third person of the Trinity. "For the father cannot be grasped. But because of God's love and goodness towards us and because he can do all things, he goes so far as to grant those who love him the privilege of seeing him…For " what is impossible for men is possible for God." (St. Irenaeus)

The Ten Commandments, the Sermon on the Mount, the Christian baptism, the religion in the early Catholic Church was designed to spread the glory of God and the apostolic faith that was shared with humanity from Jesus's teachings and His disciples. The Catholic Church uses Gospel stories and brief formulas, which were largely intended for baptism. Baptismal candidates could memorize these formulas and practice their teachings. As the Catholic Church spread throughout the world, gaining many new followers, it required a common language to express the church's beliefs.

The Apostles' Creed was one aspect of a common language, allowing unification between Catholics worldwide and ensuring all Catholics shared the same beliefs. At its core, the Apostles' Creed is a profession of faith in God and His teachings, and it includes articles about each of the three persons of the Holy Trinity. The Apostles' Creed serves as a concise summary of Catholics' beliefs and the core aspects of the Scripture and God's teachings. To recap, the Apostles' Creed is attributed to some of the earliest missionary followers of Jesus Christ, distilling the fundamental basics of what it means to be a Catholic and follow in the teachings of God. The creed acts as a concise summary of His teachings and is deeply rooted in Scripture. By reciting the Apostles' Creed, we can feel a sense of unity and community with fellow Catholics of every age worldwide. When we recite the Apostles' Creed during Mass, we end the creed saying "Amen," our declaration of affirmation and confirmation. We, the assembled faithful of Christ, recite the creed as it is our shared belief. While the creed is not our entire faith, it mentions fundamental truths we believe and surmises the teachings within the Scripture. Although the Apostles' Creed was written centuries ago, it still plays an important role in the Catholic Church, allowing us to reflect on the words and praise the glory of God. The Catechism of the Catholic Church defines a creed as a symbol of faith. The Apostles' Creed is one of the prayers of the Rosary and gets it's name because it is considered a summary of each Apostle's faith.

The Apostles' Creed is also known as "Apostolicum," a profession of faith used in the Catholic Church. Previously, the Apostles' Creed was said to be composed by the 12 Apostles. Now, the creed is thought to have been developed from initial interrogations of catechumens, people receiving instructions to be baptized. An early version of what later became the Apostles' Creed, called the "Old Roman Creed," was in use as early as the second century (Kelly, Creeds, 101). The earliest written form of this creed is found in a letter that Marcellus of Ancyra wrote in Greek to Julius, the bishop of Rome, about AD 341.

The current Apostles' Creed resembles aspects of the baptismal creed used in Roman churches in the 3rd and 4th centuries. The Apostles' Creed reached its final iteration in the early 7th century. Over time, the Apostles' Creed replaced other baptismal creeds and was determined as the official profession of faith for the Catholic Church during Pope Innocent III's tenure. The Catholic version of the Apostles' Creed is used daily in personal worship and during baptisms. While the Apostles' Creed is regularly used in the church, it is also an excellent creed for personal reflection and prayer. Additionally, the Apostles' Creed is also used as a measure or rule of faith, as its articles are deeply rooted in the Catholic tradition and Scripture. When reciting the Apostles' Creed, Catholics throughout the world can be confident that they are professing beliefs shared by the whole Catholic Church.

The Apostles' Creed also helps safeguard the Catholic faith and defend it from heresy and certain challenges. Looking at each article of the Apostles' Creed can help you understand the importance of the creed.

Article 1: I Believe in God, the Father Almighty, Creator of Heaven and Earth. The first article of the Apostles' Creed affirms the existence of God and declares that God is a true God, meaning he is one God but in three persons known as the Holy Trinity. The Holy Trinity is made of the Father,

Son and Holy Spirit. The first article also states that God created everything within our universe.

Article 2: And in Jesus Christ, His Only Son, Our Lord.

The second article reaffirms that Jesus is God's son and that he is divine. The term "Lord" itself implies divinity as it is ascribed to God, so using the word "Lord" in reference to Jesus Christ directly relates the Son to divinity. Jesus's name comes from Hebrew and translates to "God saves," meaning that Jesus is our Savior.

Article 3: Who Was Conceived by the Power of the Holy Spirit and Born of the Virgin Mary.

This article affirms that Jesus Christ has human nature in the sense that he was born of a human mother, the Virgin Mary. At the same time, despite being born of a human mother, Jesus also has divine nature because he was born of the Holy Spirit and not a human father. Jesus Christ is considered both man and God, fully divine and fully human.

Article 4: He suffered under Pontius Pilate, was crucified, died, and was buried. The human nature of Christ could feel pain and actually die, and he did on Good Friday.

Article 5;He Descended Into Hell. The Third Day He Arose Again From the Dead. Jesus did not descend into the Hell of the damned where Satan resides. Instead, "hell" was a term used by early Catholics to describe the place of the dead. While Jesus died and went to the place of the dead, this states that on the third day, he rose again,

coming back from the dead due to his divine power. Jesus Christ returned from the dead in a risen and glorified body.

Article 6: He Ascended Into Heaven and Is Seated at the Right Hand of God the Father Almighty.

Article 7: He Will Come Again to Judge the Living and the Dead.

The seventh article confirms that there will be the Second Coming of Jesus Christ at the end of the world to judge the living and the dead. The Second Coming of Christ is known as the Day of Reckoning or Judgement Day, where God will judge the living and the dead and open His arms to His believers. In the Catholic faith, we believe that there is an immediate judgment of a person upon their death to determine if they will ascend into Heaven based on their life. There is also a general judgment of all of God's children during the Second Coming.

Article 8: I Believe in the Holy Spirit. The eighth article reminds us all that God is a triune God, meaning he exists in three persons known as the Holy Trinity, consisting of God the Father, the Son and the Holy Spirit. Each of these persons is distinct but equal in divinity to one another.

Article 9: The Holy Catholic Church, the Communion of Saints.

Catholics believe that the Church is an essential aspect of our lives and a way for us to celebrate the glory of God. Catholic churches are divine spaces where we may come together to learn the work of God and spread His message.

Article 10: The Forgiveness of Sins. Jesus Christ came to the world and gave his life for our sins. The forgiveness of sins is a fundamental belief of all Catholics. We are imperfect beings who will sin throughout our lives, but God still loves us and grants us forgiveness through baptism, confession and the Sacrament of Penance. God teaches us that, despite our sins, we can seek forgiveness and lead a life in His light.

Article 11: The Resurrection of the Body. In the Catholic faith, the human form is a union of the soul and body, meaning that death is only a temporary separation of the soul and body until the Second Coming of Christ, General Judgement and the resurrection of the dead. The just and righteous will ascend to Heaven with body and soul.

Article 12: And in Life Everlasting. Jesus Christ, our Lord and Saviour died, so must humans, as we are only mortals. As Jesus rose again, so shall humans, thanks to the Glory of God. Death is how we cross from our human life into the next. When we die, immediate private judgment occurs, and Christ judges our soul to determine if we are particularly virtuous. Even if we have sinned, if we profess our faith, seek forgiveness and live a virtuous life, God will allow us to ascend into Heaven.

Every man is inspired , at least implicitly, by a vision of man and his destiny, from which he derives the point of reference for its judgment, its hierarchy of values, its line of conduct. Most societies have formed their institutions in the recognition of a certain preeminence of man over things. Only the divinely revealed religion has clearly recognized man's origin and destiny in God, the Creator and Redeemer. The Church invites political authorities to measure their judgment and decisions against the inspired truth about God and man. Societies do not recognize this vision or reject it to seek its own criteria or borrow its vision from some other ideology. Mankind in general does not admit that one can defend an objective criterion of good and evil. History has shown that the powers that be are arrogant to themselves as to right and wrong. Theirs is a collective totalitarian power view of man and his destiny. It is a world based view with an objective of One World Order that rejects the spiritual in favour of the secular.

Whilst the Church has its creed and Canon Law, it is not to be confused in any way with the political community. The Mother Church in accord with the Vatican is both the sign of safeguard and the transcendent character of the human person. The Church respects and encourages the political freedom and responsibility of the citizen. It is part of the Church's mission "to pass moral judgments even in matters related to politics, whenever the fundamental; rights of man or the salvation of souls requires it. This means she may use rules in accord with the Gospel for the welfare of men according to the diversity of times and circumstances. "

It is noticeable today that the Church has become more evangelical in its approach to all matters pertaining to mankind, more ecumenical in the concept and principle that Christians who belong to different Christian denominations should work together. Many of its Canon Law however are not in my opinion, keeping with the times, and in truth are ever changing spiritual laws. Nevertheless it is willing to listen to opposing moral justifications by those like myself who may be considered outside the bounds of embracing the sacraments in the practice of the Catholic faith. The commandments still apply as they did in the Old Testament, but New Testament rules have been broken by practicing Catholic over a lifetime and it must be said that most Christian denominations, once Roman Catholic from their inception, have set off on their own course of religiosity because they could not accept the tight rules of the Church as it relates to the sacraments in particular. Christian prayer is the crux of all that the Church advocates: "Great is the mystery of faith!" The Church professes this mystery in the Apostles Creed, and celebrates it in the sacramental liturgy, so that the life of the faithful may be conformed to Christ in the Holy Spirit to the glory of God the Father. This mystery, then, requires that the faithful believe in it, that they celebrate it, and that they live from it in a vital and personal relationship with the living and true God. This relationship is prayer. " For me prayer is a surge of the heart;

it's a simple look onwards to heaven, it is a cry for recognition and of love, embracing both trial and joy." (St. Therese of Lisieux).

Prayer is the rising of one's mind and heart to God or the requesting of good things from God. But when we pray, do we speak from the heights of pride and will, or "out of the depths" of a humble and contrite heart? "He who humbles himself will be exalted."(Luke 18:9-14), humility is the foundation of prayer. As St. Gregory of Nazianzus said:' " It is the union of the entire holy and royal Trinity...with the whole human spirit." It is the grace of the kingdom in the New Covenant, the living relationship of mankind with their Father who is good beyond measure. The life of prayer is the habit of being in the presence of the thrice- God and in communion with him. This communion is always possible, through Baptism, we have already been united with Christ (Rom 6:5).

CHAPTER 12.

THE CREDO

Prayer is Christian in so far as it is communion with Christ and extends throughout the Church, which is his Body. Its dimensions are of Christ's love. Even after losing through 'sin' man remains an image of his Creator, and retains the desire for the one who calls him into existence. All religions bear witness to man's essential search for God. Man may forget his Creator or hide far from his face; he may run after idols or accuse the deity of having abandoned him; yet the living and true God tirelessly calls each person to the mysterious encounter known as prayer. In prayer, the faithful find God's initiate love always comes first; our own first step is always a response. As God gradually reveals himself and reveals man to himself, prayer appears as a reciprocal call, a covenant drama. Through words and actions, this drama engages the heart. It unfolds throughout the whole history of salvation.

So it is that modern day men to practice his belief of Christianity still need a daily tract to run on, and in this from the early days of the Church to now, there has always been prayer, there has always been a creed. A prayerful mission statement if you will for the faithful to follow, and from this participation in the holy sacrifice of the Mass and the communion of Saints. A united participation in the receiving of grace through the taking of the Eucharist during the Mass celebration. It has always been the way of the Catechism of the Catholic Church since the Apostles wrote the Gospels and St. Paul spread the message, sowing the seeds of redemption throughout the earth, which has been recalling man back to God ever since.

Be it said that whilst I have delved into the Catechism of the Catholic Church, its sacramental rituals and doctrines of faith and moral, I have barely scratched the surface of the in-depth study that one might undertake to have a more broad understanding of this faith in embracing the life of living things like, social moral, community stewardship, political and world views on matters of disease, war and peace, to name but a few.

So it is that I have written my version of the credo of the Church as it relates to my own Catholic indoctrination reflecting the journey I've taken thus far towards eternal light written in the hope that one day I may fully embrace the teachings of the scaffolding that clings to my soul (to draw an analogy,) like that of builders use for their safety on an unfinished building. Their aim is to complete the structure as to the plan of the Architect. I am also mindful that I am at this time in the spiritual plan of the building that has been designed by my Creator Architect that this builder can't build to his specifications.

So I now resolve to continue to trust in the slow work of God, to adhere to the mission statement of my own Credo whilst not fully embracing that of the Apostles Creed. Whilst I may well mouth the words aloud in a Mass service with a connotation of belief and being present, I somehow can not reconcile all of this prayer of the faithful in its present form to my conscious belief. Nor can I reconcile the teachings of the Canon Law to the fullest when it comes to personal reconciliation and absolution by a priest in order to obtain forgiveness and the receiving of the Eucharist in the Mass celebration, as I have alluded to in this book. But it must be added that I am working on it despite the fact that much of my life must change to a great degree if I am to fully embrace what the Apostles' Creed mission of the Church dictates. The least I can do is ask you dear reader to pause for a moment and to pray for me in this regard.

It was a calamity of tragic circumstances, the marriage breakdown, divorce, suicide, and the sexual abuse of one of my kin by a man of the cloth that drove me to drink alcoholically. This in turn led me down the path of ruin and ultimately into a catastrophic collapse and ultimately a rehab unit. It seemed to me that I had been abandoned by all including God and there was no way out. In time the slow work of God did work a miracle of sorts, I began to recover. For it came within a cry for help which led me to walk the Camino de Santiago and of course Alcoholics Anonymous.

The Camino Way opened up a plethora of creative inspiration which has resulted in my writing poetry, novels and recording of my songs. In turn AA led me by way of this creative expression to the belief in a Higher power of my own understanding which has floated my spiritual boat through the past 15 years of attending to the Steps of the AA programme in my life . It has been my Church and my fellowship with fellow Alcoholics God centred. But now has come the crunch, as I work to get some balance back into the logical belief as it relates to my former Catholic teaching after coming from a dark place, to embracing Church doctrine with my creative belief in God. It is with this 'belief' in mind that I write my own current Credo.

I believe in an Infinite Intelligence that I choose to call God,
the Creator of all.
I believe in the manifestation of a Risen Christ.
I believe in praying through Mary, Christ's mother.
I believe in celebrating The Mass and the Eucharist.
I believe in the Christ' consciousness of the Communion of Saints
I believe that our defects of character are forgiven.
I believe in Christ's Last Supper, death and resurrection.
I believe in the Trinity, and the grace granted for our salvation.
I believe that there is a place in the afterlife for all humanity.
Amen.

Now this is not exactly in keeping with the Catholic faith's liturgy of the Word, but it is enough right now for me to participate in the Mass celebration and accept that God forgives me by my intentions. That in the celebration of the Mass there is enough recognition of forgiveness granted through the word and general congregational confession and my willingness to ask forgiveness, that absolves me from my 'sin' at that time. Now that does not excuse me from all that I should do in my power to seek what a Church tribunal might do to render null and void my former marriage, accept my current relationship within the bounds of its moral validity, or indeed accept me for who and what I have become m in the eyes of the Lord. Church current law to determine my purpose within the bounds of the Faith of my fathers Holy faith is not my call, but that of the Church representatives who may or may not consider my case to practice the faith in accord with what is now written within the Catholic Church doctrine as opposed to what I know and practice.. Like a critical court case the preparation for my part is not something to be treated lightly and will take a lot of consideration by me before I face the jury and the judgment.

For I may well choose to ignore it all and carry on as I now practice the faith and my steps in the AA programme of life.

Should I however be resigned to letting go all that I deem as necessary to my mental, spiritual and physical wholeness in favour of practicing the faith as the Church now rules, then without a nullification of all my past life ,as laid down by a Catholic tribunal, it would mean that I would be no better off than living a life of a eunuch.like that of a priest. Or possibly a religious recluse destined to wander the earth in search of a home. Still worse, a madman of a kind wishing to be freed of his ego, who mutters to himself all day, like the Dutch Rembrandt Dutch did : " Vanity of vanities and all is vanity." Better still, live the stance of St Augustine before he gave himself up to God he prayed: "Lord, make me pure...but not yet."

For now it is best to free myself of this cursed book and hand it all over to you, to the Universe, to God, before I am inspired to act or write any further on the matter. In the meantime, I'll just say my Credo of the Mass.

The Liturgy of the Word

By hearing the word proclaimed in worship, the faithful again enter into uttering dialogue between God and the covenant people, a dialogue sealed in the sharing of the Eucharistic food.

First there is a reading of the day from a Missal ..the bookcase containing an assortment of text from old prayer books and devotional pamphlets. After the reading the congregation responds; " Thanks be to God." After this reading a cantor sings or says a Biblical Psalm. Sundays or certain other feast days of Saints, a second reading is down with the same response as the first reading. The Assembly then stands for a Gospel revelation from Christ's teachings. It is considered a welcome and begins with the priests introduction : " A reading of the Holy Gospel according to (Matthew, Mark, Luke or John)." There is a pregnant pause after the reading to reflect on the words of the point of the Liturgy. Then the priest: responds; "This is the word (Gospel) of the Lord. The assembly replies : Praise be to you, Lord Jesus Christ." The priest then preaches a homily; a religious discourse that is intended primarily for spiritual edification rather than doctrinal instruction. This is then followed by the Apostles Creed:

I believe in God,
The Father Almighty,
Make of heaven and earth,
Of all things visible and invisible.

I believe in one Lord Jesus Christ
The Only Begotten Son of God
Born of the Father before all ages,
God from God, Light from light,
True God from true God, begotten, not made, consubstantial
With the Father: Through him all things were made.
For us men and for our salvation
He came down from heaven.
And by the Holy Spirit was incarnate
Of the Virgin Mary, And became man.

For our sake he was crucified
Under Pontius Pilate,
He suffered death and was buried,
And he rose on the third day
In accordance with the Scriptures.
He ascended into heaven
And is seated at the right hand of the Father
He will come to judge the living and the dead
And his kingdom will have no end.

I believe in the Holy Spirit,
The Lord and giver of life,
Who proceeds from the Father and the Son,
who is worshiped and glorified,
Who had spoken through the prophets.
I believe in one, holy Catholic and apostolic Church.
I confess one baptism for the forgiveness of sins
and I look forward to the resurrection of the dead
And the life of the world to come. Amen.

In the Communion Rite of the Mass The Lord's prayer is recited.
And the priest concludes with'" Let us offer each other as a sign of peace." The Assembly offers each other a sign.
The priest concludes : " The peace of the Lord be with you all."
And the respondents " And with your Spirit."
The Mass is concluded with a blessing.
"May Almighty bless you, in the name of the Father.
The Son and there Holy Spirit."

The priest concludes:" The Mass is ended,
Go forth and serve the Lord."

Doug McPhillips, poet, singer, songwriter, author, commenced his journey of discovery over a decade ago after life changing experiences.

The many tracks he has traversed throughout the Northern Hemisphere and down under in New Zealand and Australia has resulted in the facts and fictions of this novel.

Doug has written eight novels, a book of poems, a travel guide and two albums of his songs all inspired by his adventurers.

www.caminoway.com.au

In parts of Africa, babies may be named according to when they were born or where they were born. In many cases parents name their babies, or give them their first name.

In Australian Aboriginal culture babies names partake of the personality which elders designate. The name seems to bear much the same relation to the personality as the shadow or image does to the sentient body. Names are not symbols but projections of an identity which is well known in the flesh. A name may be given based of elements specific to that person which may include significant happenings to or by the person , or a characteristic that defines that person.

It is common for people of eastern philosophy, particularly Hindus, to give a new born a name based on a horoscope, usually provided by an astrologer. The astrologer determines the sound a name should begin with and the family will choose a name based on that sound. It is common for people to have nicknames among close friends and family.

Among Orthodox Jews, the first choice is often the paternal grandfather (if he is no longer alive). On the other hand, Sephardi Jews often name their children for someone who might still be living (again, traditionally the firstborn is named after the paternal grandfather).

Naming a child, popularly referred to in "Christening" is usually through the baptism ceremony, especially Catholic culture, and to a lesser degree among those Protestants who practice infant baptism.

All children born to earth are "Children of God" irrespective of how they are named. Something to think about right?

www.ingramcontent.com/pod-product-compliance
Lightning Source LLC
Chambersburg PA
CBHW060522010526
44107CB00060B/2651